Arthur Lynch

Approaches

Vol. III

Arthur Lynch

Approaches
Vol. III

ISBN/EAN: 9783337051341

Printed in Europe, USA, Canada, Australia, Japan

Cover: Foto ©ninafisch / pixelio.de

More available books at **www.hansebooks.com**

APPROACHES

THE POOR SCHOLAR'S QUEST OF A MECCA

A Novel

IN THREE VOLUMES

BY

ARTHUR LYNCH

Author of "Modern Authors"

VOL. III

EDEN, REMINGTON & CO PUBLISHERS
LONDON AND SYDNEY.

1892

[*All rights reserved*]

CONTENTS.

IDYLLS.

CHAPTER I. 1
Broken Words.
Faith.
A Nimbus round the Form.
A Simple School Girl yet.
The Losing of a Kiss.

CHAPTER II. 31
A Poke Bonnet.

CHAPTER III. 39
The Weight at the Heart.
Solitude, Life, Death, Love, Truth.

CHAPTER IV. 43
The Transcendental Self.
"The Spilling Tears."
"Apologia."
From Girlhood.
The Talisman.
The Top of the Hill.
"Auld Robin Gray."
A Nation before Us.
"Sudden a Thought came like a Full Blown Rose."
The Outset.

CHAPTER V. 76
The Growth of Faith.
Mary Neville.
Tales out of School.
"The Good Little Crock."
Neatly Tucked Up.

THE COMING HOME.

CHAPTER VI. 98
The Good Ship.
Austin.
Three Pioneers.

CHAPTER VII. 105
The Swimmer.
Hester Sterne.
Foreboding.
A Philosopher.
Dead Letters.
Physical Cultivation.

CHAPTER VIII. ... 124
Mad Waves.
On the Rocks.
The Rescue.

CHAPTER IX. 144
The Swimmer's Struggles.

CHAPTER X. 151
Accounts Rendered.
Mary.

CHAPTER XI. 162
"For the Child's Sake."
"She is Dead."
For Mercy—Forgiveness.

BETWEEN TWO LIVES.

CHAPTER XII. 185
"Truth is the Innermost Kernel of all that is Great."
Material Obstacles.
Enduring Structures.
Analysis of Love.

CHAPTER XIII. 214
The Sweet Puritan.
Yes, Austin.
The Mignonette.
The "Orbed Drop."

IDYLLS.

CHAPTER I.

Now in Tarylvale once again Austin felt the old charm refreshing him and with its quiet restoration making recompense for many wearing months.

He walked with his mother about the garden. There was something of desertion about it when he remembered the picture of the children playing there.

His mother had spoken to him almost for the first time about her own past life, and described how she had been brought up almost without playmates, and if almost without pleasures, yet almost without cares.

But that, Austin, was no solace. I was yearning not for pleasures,—I will not say for cares, but for work I could give myself up to, to do something—useful—honourable —even if pains, and cares, solicitude should come. Reading was a great resource, but I read irregularly, wildly, for myself. The books I read led me on to search and push my own thoughts. It was metaphysical.

Hence these tears, said Austin, grimly.

And as a young girl I used at times to find an exquisite pleasure in solitude, for then my thoughts were purest and deepest. And every tree and every flower and every leaf and every pebble was a thing not merely to be seen or felt, but leading on to something inscrutable—fathomless in mystery; and looking at the sunsets as we see them here, with all the feeling of the grandeur and the awe that raises one, and then the sunrise when earth and every living thing is stirred with a quick tide of life, my feelings used to sweep out almost in passion—God is there, and endless life. . . . And when your father brought me to this house I felt, even secluded as my life has been, that my life was filled and my destiny achieved. I think, if I were so to say it, that I was more emotional than intellectual. Your father instructed me in faith, and all that my mind and soul had craved for was there. It was complete. . . . O Austin, the pain and the grief came soon enough, the visit of death that you scarcely can remember. . . . and, Austin, *you* have grieved me.

I have not been altogether at peace with myself, he said.

O Austin, think while there is yet time and do not do so wrong a thing. Your father built on you. What disappointment he suffered it was respect for your feelings made him conceal. Think Austin—unsuccessful in this, unsuccessful in that, talents, opportunities wasted. Your wild talk and your hopeless ideas distress me. Without an aim, without a religion, without a God, one could say, tossed hither and thither.

Well, but Austin! Moody, solitary, eating your heart out with wild fancies and still losing your hold ever more and more on purpose. This is a wretched outcome for years of patient hope. Your father clung to hope through it all. He fell ill, Austin, then came the last. You know what did it. He thought only of duty. No word of complaint. And when he saw that the end must come—Well, Austin, your fate was never from his mind. He talked with you, what he said I do not know, but this much I know that even then his own feelings, his own distress, he would conceal and think only of your happiness. He entreated you while there is yet time, by an effort which he knew that you could make Austin, now even now, to retrieve your lost position, even though you dated from his death-bed your salvation. He might with the thoughts of that, while you saw him sinking have wrung a promise from you that would have assured him peace. His mind was too noble for that. But, Austin, stronger than such a promise should your duty be, and if he entreated you only, the thousand times the more should every good and generous feeling urge you.

She ceased. Her manner quiet at first had increased in earnestness and pathos.

Austin felt the undercurrent too.

She looked up·at him, but could distinctly read nothing.

This is not all, Austin, she continued.

You are leaving home, leaving sisters and brother, making them strangers, leaving me. It seems—to me—for ever—to me—for ever —I have lately thought — the tears had flowed from her eyes before, her voice was trembling now, and she spoke very slowly, Oh it is fearful—it's no weak spirit makes me say it. O Austin come back you may— but my eyes will never see you more.

She looked at Austin again. She turned her head away. Her feelings were escaping all control.

With the wildness of despair she pleaded, but in a low broken voice, placing her hands upon his arm. Behold, Austin! I have given you your life! I have nourished you. From my knees you learned the first stumbling step. In my arms you uttered your first syllables. You have grown to manhood. From then till now in ten thousand ways your image has come to me and the depths of my heart have been given you. Now still I speak to you. A knife is put into your hand to slay me. Will you drive it home? Would you behold me in death? For this parting is—to me, death.

*   *   *   *   *

Harold and Susan came running to meet him.

Well Harold, old fellow, said he taking the youngster by the hand, and are you an optimist? Do you enjoy life, Harold?

Hurrah! cried Harold.

Hurrah! You give me hope, this natural cheer of yours. Where have you been?

Out riding—grand—took the pony over that big log near Ben Church's gate, you know. It was fine. He ran away from Ted Dunstan's.

That was a cowardly thing to do, said Austin laughing.

Faith is coming, said Susan who saw this

chance of getting in a say. I got a telegram. She's coming to-night.

Faith! Ah. She'll be a nice companion for you, eh? Good child she is.

Good child! They grow, Austin!

Austin drove Susan and Harold in to meet Faith.

That interesting being kissed Susan affectionately like old friends, shook hands with Harold heartily, and when Austin sprang out and ran forward to greet her as he used to do, her face was well contained as she extended her hand quietly, and taking Susan round the waist marched off not without a certain dignity.

They grow! said Austin half-laughingly and half-admiringly, and sat quietly, not uninterested, whilst Susan and Faith chatted away on girl's topics, during the homeward drive.

The two school girls had much to say to each other, and Austin and Harold were much edified, and talked confidentially between themselves.

Girls are right enough in their way, Harold began sententiously.

What's that, Harold? said Faith. Harold, if you are not gallant—I'll kiss you! We'll kiss him, Susan, now.

The youngster resisted however very stoutly.

That's all girls are good for, he explained to Austin, while very red in the face, soft nonsense and talk. When it comes to shooting, or riding, or playing cricket, or kicking a football, or climbing a tree, they're nowhere!

And so in good humour the party reached home.

At tea, and in the evening afterwards, there were many changes to observe in Faith.

His eyes began to follow her as Susan soon remarked, but Faith was all unconscious.

The two girls withdrew early.

Faith! said Harold nodding his head in the direction of her room.

Pretty?

Yes, she'll do. But—she's quite like a little lady!

Could one trace out the dainty little nine year old in the young lady who was growing up?

The next day she appeared in a new dress, and treated Austin with great reserve. But soon she became more friendly, and, in the evenings, played. One could admire her as she sat at the instrument, slight and girlish still, with easy strength of movement. Felicity of health was there. Her face was glowing now. She had been laughing with Susan and kissing her, and now as she composed herself, her eyes still twinkled and the soft flush o'erspread her cheek.

Flowers and fruits, the pleasant fields, the changing shapes,
And Nature in her glorious power, the mood sublime, are truly fit poetic themes.
But now with curious regard, nay, with the shade of very present reverence,
Do I behold each human form;
For who can measure here the limit and the play of will and force and passion? Who not keenly feel, barren all else without, the touch of human fellowship, the mutual fire divine?

. . . . . .

And who is this radiant form?
What sweet mystic here?

APPROACHES.

And what the mysteries beneath those steadfast eyes?
A maiden, she, with simple talk of things beseeming a
    sweet maiden's life,
Of books and studies—household cares mayhap;
The bright awakening thoughts of life, its many coloured
    guise.
The eager eyes on knowledge and its opening world, I see,
The glowing and the pensive mood;
A mind quite deeply touched by wisdom from within;
Sweet mind still chastened by the present awe that looms
    in Nature's life.

.   .   .   .   .   .

And now once more do I behold and wonder in a new
    delight.
For graceful hands have swept the chords and won from
    obdurate things a living voice.
Mine eyes are closed, my soul is lulled,
                I dream.
And now the pictures of the mind stand clear,
They vanish—and succeed them newer scenes,
Through all impressed a sadness, strange and sweet.
O how clinging to the heart, the touch of human fellow-
    ship,
Those eyes, how wistful, and the sound of voices gone.
Still fall the notes, their pathos—and the pain that now
    I feel—now—
Me hath the struggling of my heart awaked?
The music hath it ceased?
What witchery is this? What deep magician art?
And where the mystic with the mystic power?
A maiden with a calm and gentle face,
A nimbus round the form,
And yet—fully humanly—'tis *thee* I see!

.   .   .   .

A radiant presence, said Austin in perplexity. If I allow her to assume her little sovereignty, I never will be able to approach the little goddess. Therefore I will break down her little barriers of dignity at once.

The two girls were quite earnest in their book with heads bent close together. Austin strode up and taking Faith by the waist laid his head on hers. She sprang to her feet, but there were too many blushes to be wholly dignified.

He held her hands and while, half with laughing and half with blushing, the dimples came into her cheeks and the steadfast eyes began to glow, she declared that it was not fair at all.

Pooh, he said, laughing, we must preserve a human sort of bearing. That celestial mode of yours was making me feel cold, as though I were a being of a lower sphere.

The red lips and the sparkling eyes were wonderful, and Austin laughed at her indignation as she marched with Susan from the room.

Sweet she was, and fresh, and graceful.

The nimbus round the form did not vanish on a nearer view. Austin, interested, half laughing, noticed all sorts of little things about her, foolish enough to relate.

The pale patient face he saw was lighted up at times and glowed with a warm suffusement. The steadfast eyes could play with twinkling lights, but their gaze was like an angel's. The "locked-up little mouth" could wreath and arch dimples play about the cheeks.

Health dwelt in her. She carried Nature's benediction on her form. A godly little temple, he used to say, when he gazed on her, and felt a gladness to stand beside her.

Faith bore her graces neither meekly nor proudly. Her unconsciousness it was that gave her a charm. A Vandal only could beflatter her. Her white dress, for it was warm summer, charming! Her dark dress none the less, and she looked best in grey. It was that he remembered her in when she had sat at the table long ago with the lamp light on her head puzzling over her arithmetic and had brought the book to him.

He noticed many more frivolous things than this, noticed the dainty play of ankle as she had waited a moment for Susan at the gate; noticed the simmering smiles as she had done her hair up once in ultra-fashionable style and tossed her head, running away to hide herself again.

He drove Faith and Susan long drives and walked with them long walks, and it seemed as though her light elastic step could carry her for hours with never a thought of tiring.

And he noticed too how the sweet face grew grave, the steadfast eyes partook of deeper lights, when his voice grew low and earnest. When Susan too, unimaginative child, tired of Austin's talk, insisted upon driving, and made the horses bolt down hill, and shrieked with a furious terror, and Austin had to press every muscle to save a smash, Faith had sat serious but still as a block, then smiled, and was the first to tease him into laughing.

Austin began to lose his studies to be near the little school girl and somewhat interrupted hers. She ran away from him, shut herself up, slipped out of the room when she saw him coming, and he was brought to begging for her music now. No. It was not so very wrong to lose his studies for a week or so he thought. This would be a sweet picture to take away and presently he would resume them with energy renewed.

Susan began to think, and confide her own misgivings too to Harold.

Tut, nonsense, said the youngster. Susan might as well have told him that Austin was beginning to take a growing interest in the making of mud pies.

Very well, then, we'll see, and Susan nodded her head up and down, his eyes follow her everywhere. I wonder Faith never notices it herself. Even when he is reading like a great bear you'd think all by himself— I saw him look up every time she turned her head.

Pooh. Girl's talk. What silly creatures girls are, and Harold nodded his head too, and went away with speculative rumination as to what particularly such beings were created for.

But Faith's a girl, Austin had said to him laughingly.

H'm. Well she's different, she's got some sense about her and understands things, but Susan she stouches every game almost as soon as you begin to play, and can't bowl a ball; I let her throw at the wicket, but she can't do that; can't climb a tree for a bird's nest—!

Faith a simple school girl yet; he had a little programme planned out; he would take her out for drives here and there, and they would go long walks together This was for her good. Then he would instruct her. She would read Spencer's little book on Education! and he had a plan for teaching her algebra. Then in the evenings she would play music. Faith was, however, more difficult to please. When he asked her if she wanted to be a "good little girl" she answered somewhat curtly "No;" and when he asked her to come for a drive or for a walk she coolly weighed the pros and cons. These things were disconcerting. Here was a schoolgirl—not defying him with flashing eyes, simply unconscious of any exercise of power. He betook himself to his books and left her alone, severely. She seemed to experience no sense of coldness, perhaps thought it natural he should wish to read there undisturbed. Then he forsook his studies and the schoolgirl said she had heard he was a dreadfully hard worker, and smiled; and he explained carefully that he wanted to take a little rest before sailing away—for ever!

He laughed at his own perturbation; good little girl, he said.

Nevertheless Susan was nodding her head more sagaciously than ever, and even Harold muttered "foolish" to himself.

Austin was angry for being so pleased when she said "yes" to a walk or drive.

When the two girls sat at the piano and looked to each other and smiled to give the start and played the piece together—surely there is no sight more charming than two innocent fresh beings in all the grace of girlhood sitting so together and making mutual melody.

There was something idyllic in this present life and the days were gliding by. Soon he would be called to sterner things; meanwhile the little shepherdess was interesting.

How old are you, Faith? he questioned as he looked with a smile at the grave little personage beside him.

H'm, let me see. I'm sixteen. Past sixteen, Austin.

For some things I might have thought you more, for others less. The grave patient look and the little locked-up lips, Faith, are almost beyond your years but,—glancing at the girlish figure—yes the colour of cheeks and the free light step would make me think you still a little girl. Tell me about your reading, Faith? That's good to talk of, eh? One is afraid of appearing frivolous before that resolute little countenance. Do not pout though, or you'll throw away your wand. You've read a good deal?

No, not much. To you I ought to say hardly anything, indeed, for I have many things to attend to, and with music, French, drawing and other lessons I have hardly any time left to myself.

Quite a round of fashionable accomplishments. What books are you fond of?

I think I like history best, said Faith.

History, then, and not mathematics? The delicate sex love the concrete, eh? Not algebra?

No. I never could learn it. I never could get any one to explain to me what it all meant and what was the use of it all.

And yet you would not let me. Faith Shenstone there is a wicked pride in you. Well then, physiology?

No, of course not. We only learn useful things, the teachers say.

No doubt geography?

Yes, replied Faith in her peculiar sort of faithful way, long strings of names. We hunt them up in our atlases. They ask what and where are the following? and some of them we have to search for ever so long.

Still the reward is great! And grammar, too, no doubt, and Latin and Greek?

Grammar and Latin of course, but not

Greek, Austin. Greek is only useful if you're going in for medicine, isn't it? inquired Faith looking up.

Very well, what part of speech is *therefore?*

Therefore,—a compound illative conjunction; Austin, you see I know that.

Good. You take your lessons to heart I see. But what's the meaning of that word—illative, is it?

Illative, h'm, O go on, Austin. I'm not going to answer all your questions.

But you know the derivation of it, surely.

No, not of that word, but of most of them. We learn up the derivation of every word in the poems we have set.

Good, I see you go deep into the matter; deeper than John Keats used to go or Robin at his plough. You are being beautifully schooled all round, Faith. But to return to the history, how is it that you like that subject best?

Oh, then I sometimes read for myself and like to picture the people as I think they would be, and the times in which they lived, and their costumes, and their strange beliefs and superstitions. It seems so hard to realize that they walked about the earth just as we do, so different in many things and yet so like in others.

Yes, said Austin, it is strange. How very absurd some of those customs and beliefs and superstitions were! Ah. Now tell me who was the man who threw the sacred chickens overboard.

That was, no. Let me see. H'm, no. No I have forgotten.

To be sure, said Austin, and Faith was wondering what was keeping him amused in this conversation. And you have never heard about George Fox?

No, who was he, Austin?

You know all about James the First, though, don't you, Faith, and the date of his accession?

Yes, of course said Faith quite eagerly. We know all the dates. They are always being drilled into us, so that we can't help learning. We learn out of a small book where all the dates for everything are given at the side. It takes up too much lesson time though and the teachers won't let us read what we like. They only give us the important events, such as the accession and deaths of sovereigns, and the battles, and whatever comes into the examination work. But I have at home books of biographies of great men, and also Plutarch's lives. Mama bought these for me.

Your mama's a treasure. So much for history—what else do you read. Think now, Faith! What other reading have you when you get those few spare moments to yourself?

Well, said Faith, hesitatingly, I have read some novels—but I don't count that—not many though. Sometimes I think I ought to be at my lessons and Miss Sharp says it wastes time reading that stuff that is not true.

To be sure, said Austin, they are not true. It is the accession of kings and queens, and the battles, and other important events, and the dates, that are true. The dates especially. Well?

And then perhaps mama might not like me to read many novels. Do you think there is any harm in it, Austin?

Let me hear first what you have read, Faith. All of them.

I have really read very few now that I think, Uncle Tom's Cabin I have read over and over again. Is not Eva a sweet character, Austin? said Faith, and her eye softened as she looked up.

Sweet indeed, Faith.

And old Uncle Tom himself, isn't he a good old fellow, and poor St. Clair. Faith became now at once more animated and gentler in her manner and as she described the book with sympathetic touches of detail. Austin remained silent and thoughtful.

Yes, good indeed, said he in answer to her question.

And what others have you read?

Let me see. Old Curiosity Shop,—Barnaby Rudge, and Ivanhoe, Princess of Thule, and Lorna Doone of course — Have you read Lorna Doone?

No, is it good?

Good, yes! And it is told so well. The words are all simple—odd, quaint, some of them, but so happily they come in. The wind was so strong it made the blackbirds look bigger! And the description of Lorna, coming down the valley with the light in the west behind her from the setting sun, and the primroses looked brighter as she looked at them—Oh, she is sweet—beautiful; and poor old John Ridd, he deserved her.

Very well. I will read it for the sake of Faith, and then we can talk about it together. But let me see, Jane Eyre and Thackeray's, and George Eliot's—No, perhaps, they had better come after. But, Ah! Vicar of Wakefield?

No—is it good?

A little treasure. One of the sweetest things in literature, I think; tastes of the country air, Faith, and green fields and all the warmth of home. It is an idyllic poem. You'll like that, Faith I know. And I must get you Milton's L'Allegro too. If you learn off passages in that—you need not mind the derivations this time,—they'll come back to you a hundred times —

I'm reading David Copperfield now; I would like to read all of Dickens, and —

And you have so little time! What would become of the geography and the compound illative conjunctions and the dates?

They walked happily along. Faith had given Austin her hand and their glances in each other's eyes were guileless and confiding as children's.

And do you ever read poetry, Faith?

No, I know you think I have no Soul, and Faith affected to pout as she laid a peculiar emphasis on *Soul*.

By which, you little witch, you mean quietly to laugh at me to my face.

Well, Austin, why should I read what I do not care about? said the school girl decidedly.

Certainly, you should not. It is better to be a sincere little woman, than to pretend to admire poetry. I'm seriously inclined to like you better for it.

What, you, Austin? I thought you raved about it.

Why! have you ever heard me talk of poetry?

No.

Can anyone else say so?

I don't know—but they—I thought you used to rave about it; but I don't care, I'll say what I mean. I don't see why you should be so very angry at that?

Austin laughed heartily.

Good little Faith.

However, you like Shakspeare, Faith?

No. Miss Sharp sometimes reads us passages out of the plays and she always changes her voice in such a way and puts on such a peculiar face that I can hardly keep serious.

You must learn to talk more reverently of this matter though. Read Julius Cæsar when I'm away and see how you like the character of Portia there.

After a pause he added, How do you like this? and repeated slowly some of the lines in St. Agnes Eve.

> Full on this casement shone the wintry moon,
>   And threw gules on Madeline's fair breast,
> As down she knelt for heaven's grace and boon ;
>   Rose-bloom fell on her hands together prest,
> And on her silver cross soft amethyst,
>   And on her hair a glory, like a saint :
> She seemed a splendid angel, newly drest,
>   Save wings for Heaven. Porphyro grew faint :
> She knelt, so pure a thing, so free from mortal taint.

And so he continued to quote and then growing warm, and though he held her hand scarcely noticing her presence, he repeated lines from Endymion.

> A thing of beauty is a joy for ever—
>
> . . . . . .
>
> Some flowery band to bind us to the earth
>
> . . . . . .
>
> An endless fountain of immortal drink

he said turning to Faith,

> Pouring unto us from the heaven's brink.

Yes, I like that, Austin. Did you write that ?

I ! Good Heavens, no. That's John Keats. Listen, Faith.

> Perhaps the self-same song that found a path
> Through the sad heart of Ruth, when, sick for home,
> She stood in tears amid the alien corn,

Perhaps the self-same song that found a path
Through the sad heart of Ruth, when, sick for home,
She stood in tears amid the alien corn,

Perhaps the self-same song that found a path
Through the sad heart of Ruth, when, sick for home,
She stood in tears amid the alien corn.

* * * * *

Faith was the next to take the conversation up. She had drawn two or three deep breaths too, glanced about a little uneasily, then with a decided little manner looked up.

Austin, said she, you have questioned me finely and made me tell you one thing and another; but you seem to put a barrier between yourself and everyone else.

Is that really so, Faith, I have been talking away at large.

Yes, when you talk or listen to people about something else. . . . I've noticed it, Austin.

Observant little girl, said Austin laughing.

Not only that but you seem content to be for hours, for days, by yourself, and what are you thinking of, I don't know. And—and—and—and now that you are going away altogether—

Do you approve of that?

No, indeed I do not. Nor anyone else who takes any interest in you. And your mother, Austin. No, Austin, nothing can make it right. You will go away locked up in yourself, and those who think most of you will be as if they never knew you. . . . Or perhaps you'll take some other mad freak!

What! you little shrew—talk to me like that, said he laughingly; I'll kiss you for revenge.

They were near the house now.

Austin, you have no right to talk like that. You laughed at my school lessons—and you are never serious—and you try to play on me—and—and you're never sincere, and she nodded her head in an emphasis that made him smile.

Good little Faith, but you'll kiss me all the same, and he caught her in his arms.

Let me go—you have no right—she struggled. Austin! she cried out, and Susan at that moment appeared from behind the hedge.

Austin!

The two stood there, Austin blushing and

crestfallen ; Faith blushing, and sparkling, and victorious; and Susan put her arm round her waist turned her back and bore Faith off under her wing.

H'm, kiss me indeed, said Faith, and—and laugh at me in a week. He thinks school girls have no mind of their own perhaps.

And Susan's high state of indignation over such a supposition burst all the bounds of her vocabulary, and she patronised Faith to keep up the dignity of schoolgirls.

It was by no means easy to see Faith after this.

She seemed in need of no explanations, sentimental or otherwise.

She escaped from him and seemed happy in that.

He began to chide himself for his disastrous waste of time, and with much stoical fortitude resolved that she must even do without this explanation and betook himself to books once more.

Then in her happy freedom the little maid was fresh and bright again, gained too some confidence and played for him.

Sensible little girl, she sees the matter herself, he said. I would like to know that though. Faith, we'll go for a walk this afternoon?

Yes that will be nice I think, Susan. We'll all go up Duncan's Hill.

Austin's brow darkened.

Oh well, Austin, if you only asked us from politeness, said Susan, you needn't think yourself called upon a bit. We can amuse ourselves together quite well, I think, Faith?

Faith smiled and pouted and said nothing, and took Susan round the waist and they tripped off together.

Austin took them for a drive next day to show that he was not ruffled by such inconsiderate behaviour, and on the whole deported himself so well, that when on going into the house he pulled Faith's hand to detain her, and whispered quickly in her ear—a walk to-morrow Faith? that little personage nodded graciously her head.

CHAPTER II.

How pretty Faith looks in that poke bonnet, he said to himself as she appeared radiant and fresh.

Sweet girl she is, there is no harm and no weakness after all perhaps in enjoying this gentle sway of power she has; and Faith walked demurely by his side.

He was in good humour and inclined to talk, but she did not seem to fall into step, and with the head demurely bent the poke bonnet hid her face. He exerted himself and ransacked his brain for interesting subjects, attempted to be very witty, then felt very like a fool. He could see beneath the poke bonnet only the locked up little lips, and Faith seemed occupied with absent thoughts. He might just as well talk to her through a wall—better!

He walked in the middle of the road, and she kept near the side; he tried to come closer and she walked unobservantly over tufts of grass, prodding the ground with her umbrella.

I can understand my books, he cried impatiently, when I read a passage I find the next has some connection with it. If I do my best to learn I am rewarded too by knowing something. There's an easy comfort there, a satisfactory reasonableness.

Well, Austin?

Well it isn't so in everything, he cried and stalked indignantly along.

Faith had a little difficulty in keeping pace, and presently began to fall behind. He waited and for the rest of the walk strode slowly, looking straight forward in a profoundly meditative mood. They arrived near home in silence.

Well, Austin have you worked out that problem yet?

What problem? he demanded sternly.

Why, were you not working out some mathematics that you seemed to speak so little?

She did not look up and so did not see the look he gave her.

He tried to be expressive by setting his heels firmly to mother earth, but she was occupied too in her own thoughts. He stepped forward to open the gate. Yes, he could forgive her even then—and have an explanation. He could forgive her without an explanation.

The smile beamed on his face, the two eyes would meet—the mutual connective glance. Yes in that, all that was troublous would be lost. She passed demurely through the gate and the poke bonnet hid her face. She did not see the beaming smile, the soft engaging glance—the poke bonnet hid all that—she did not see the thunder clouds that gathered on his brows. Malign poke bonnet —most villainous of gear!

He stormed furiously, and marched up Duncan's Hill and into the bush, powdering along till he was completely out of breath.

Well, well, what an unconscionable imbecile, he cried, a schoolgirl passes through a gate and doesn't look at me, and I've been meditating all the haunts of pessimism—A wayward girl—Shallow in mind, shallow in feeling. Such things have happened to me before. I've tried to strike sparks from those whose natures had no fire, and found their shallowness, their incapacity, at length. I've felt foolishly distressed and then recovered and laughed at myself for having given my heart to those who never could be stirred, and blessed then my escape. What's that Emerson says about a Collyrium to clear our eyes—Yes, that's it. Great Heavens! I've been troubled as much about these wayward little whims as if—as if—Pshaw!

Yet, playing with an idea, he said, Yes, it's wonderful how one might be drawn into delusions. He must demean himself now in a way of common sense, perhaps it was wrong to her to have taken much notice of her.

Sobered by the cold play of reason and

with an inexorable fate looming nearer that would call forth some sterner thoughts, he settled to his books again.

Faith he saw little of and when he did he treated her with a politeness that was a sort of apology to himself for any previous frivolity. He was almost ceremonious to her, and had quite forgiven her.

Seclusion and application count for much no doubt, so Faith may have concluded that in this interval he was learning much.

This was not wholly the case. Perhaps there was some misapprehension in this matter. Had something unintentional offended her? He speculated much. Such things often happened. He knew several cases of such trivial misapprehensions where the consequences were distressing—more so than one might think would flow from so slight causes.

He had read of the same in books.

Had not Pettigrew in fact, who was a sensible enough fellow as the world goes, made it into a sort of rule that misapprehensions should be *always* brought to definite explanations ? It was better just to mention something of this sort to Faith. He was sure he had never wished to give her pain. Better explain this and then settle down again quietly to study.

And then again what explanation could there be—no, he would simply banish her from his mind, the whole business was so trivial—he would simply disregard all thoughts of her and with an effort that partook of Stoic heroism he would dive into his books once more.

Then a brilliant idea struck him, he would say " good-bye " to her as though he had already gone, would perhaps even explain why, and then he would be completely undisturbed.

While still meditating this, some little time after and sitting in his study, in the garden under the shade of a tree at some distance from the house, he beheld her coming in that particular direction.

How light that balanced pose as she a moment hesitated.

Then she came towards him. Yes, he

could scarcely believe his eyes. She was actually coming towards him. Now he must speak and settle it. Every step she is forcing to take against her pride, he said; I know it; I can see by the way she walks. Every single movement that brings her nearer is absolutely forced out of her.—She stood before him and he had braced himself up to speak. She looked up. Her face was grave, somewhat subdued, the steadfast eyes —what mysteries were hid beneath that steadfast gaze. Faith he had phantasied before, did not seem to be a mere figure, a circumscribed appearance, shape, and nothing more—She was a *presence*. It was as though she came from a star, and, with a sweeping train invisible but none the less investing her, and with all the impalpable mysterious influences of that, stood there.

She seemed so now. He could not speak after all.

Austin, said Faith. The soup is getting cold. Your mother sent me to tell you. She says that you eat scarcely anything lately, and the reason is, that you don't come when it's warm. It's on the table now. Will you come? She looked at him inquiringly.

I cannot, Faith. I'm tired.

Faith looked about and seeing nothing else to say or do turned and walked quietly back again. He had the chance and he had lost it. He would run after her and take her by the hand! and—suddenly, as though tiding over some internal shock, some unexpected buffeting of pain, he sprang up, and calmly and sedately, and with admirable common sense, and with the least possible regard to Faith, repaired to his dinner and ate with a hopeful appetite.

CHAPTER III.

THEY had been sitting together, his mother and he, by the window, and she was cheerful, and content, and full of hope. She was chasing away from him the strange look that had come within the last few weeks, beneath those calm features. She was telling him that she would bravely bear up.—He had gone. But the gulph of those years, the barrier of death, the fearful desire of a message, a token, rose to her mind. She had remained at the window looking into the still western landscape. She was weeping. The brave heart had given way. He had stopped, then turned and noiselessly came back; and he took her hand in his, and pressed it, and bent on his knee and kissing her hand, looked into her face—

SOLITUDE. LIFE. DEATH. LOVE. TRUTH.

Nay, I would speak if only once and say
'Tis not from lack of sympathy,—the cold, hard, obdurate forms of selfishness and pride,
That would seclude my life and kill my feelings' genial play;
But something of another sort and higher mien,
Which calls me with resistless voice.
Oh! Let me even now withdraw myself the more
Lest the weak and tardy spirit in its weakness fall behind;
For visions do I see that all human eyes may see,
Not blinded with the dust of meaner strife—
How sweeps along the Universal life,
And wields the myriad forms of all our world,
Each moment limitless with Universal change.

I've seen in history's page and tales of old romance,
The gallant hosts and proud that glittered in the sun,
Resplendent in their pomp, and passed away;
Or haply in a pensive mood have pictured in my mind,
Where once the youthful lovers told their faith,
And in the open life of Florence seen the fair display of courtesy and grace;
And turning now with wistful gaze aside
Have felt the sadness of these streets' deserted drear.

And I have looked with curious eyes
Upon the faces I have met, along the populous highways
And remoter scattered paths, and read 'mid signs of eager life—not merely the engrossing purpose of the hour—
Infallible, the growing marks of death.

Where are they now, that splendid pomp, the city's
   pride, the fair nobility of youth,
Where is the record of this fev'rous toil, and what can
   chase away these deepening lines of death?
The mystic years, the sempiternal course, filled from the
   hours—see how they glide,
They steal in silence even now away;
The wild waves sweep past us in their course.

Thou speak'st to me of future lives, long worlds of bliss,
And seek'st to lull me, me, my wild and restless soul
   with dimmer mysteries of that which I can never
   know—
No, no, away! I grasp at what I am—
The touch of ruder contact, let it be, this stern reality
   doth solace me.

The harps I long to hold and wake to music with my
   glowing hands
Are feelings of the human heart, deep, vivid, real;
The passions; Reason's chords of power—
O let them build in magical array—
The subtle wave of delicatest thought,
The tender tone, awakening pulse of action then, and
   far away throughout the diapason swell the mighty
   songs of genius, trumpet-tongued.

This is my heaven, this earth, this only do I know;
My angels are the faces that do hover near—
Sweet words, man's strong appeal for brotherhood,
The things familiar of our daily life, the service of the
   hour—toil—bread.

And shall I halt and totter,
I alone upon the world's great vast?

Flee from the thought, tho' cowardly thy flight.
Hold to thy clew—to trace the labyrinth of doubt,
The dungeon's walls, the chambers, higher courts, and now
To palaces where science dwells,
The Truth will lead thee on through many a winding way,—
And vistas open up before thine eyes,—
On wandering—wandering to the light of day.

CHAPTER IV.

AND Austin reflecting on the adventure of the poke-bonnet was trying to discover the secret influence that could make him such a fool. Recollecting Byron's exquisite lines he concluded, not unreasonably, that it had much to do with Idleness. Once more then into his Kantean metaphysics, that Serbonian Bog, in which a whole nation might be lost, he was plunging, and not without ostensible success.

It was Faith who began to lose her dinner now, Susan observed. You silly girl, Faith, . . . , was the only comment she made— some more cherry pie.

The good mother was venting her heart as they slowly walked in the garden.

Susan and Harold presently came running up.

When are you going to bring us for a drive again, Austin, said the buxom lass, you are going away so soon now, that we won't have many more chances of getting drives. You said the next time would be the last. We'll go early and take our lunch and spend the day at Purrumbra Lake—it will be nice, eh? And you mustn't bring any of your dry old books—and get cross —

Susan?

Cross, yes! But I don't care whether you do or not. We'll go away behind the bank and take off our stockings and paddle in the water. I believe Faith would like to also, prim as she is.

Where is she? She usually comes out into the garden about this hour.

O, she's playing music, I think. There's not half the fun in her lately. But, Austin, what have you done to her? She would scarcely speak to me, and I saw tears in her eyes. What did you do?

Tears! Ho, ho. Tell me, tell me.

We were sitting together in the garden under the pear tree there, and I was watching a little wagtail that was hopping near. It was quite funny to watch it. Have you ever watched wagtails going —

Go on!

Well after a time I noticed that Faith had grown very quiet. She was sitting behind me with a book, and I thought she must have fallen asleep or something, and looked quickly round to see if she was there. And just at that moment she looked up quickly too. Her lips were on the brink of trembling and the tears were in her eyes—nearly spilling out. I looked at her and she turned her head quickly round and then I caught her round the waist and kissed her. But she would not tell me what was the matter. She choked the tears back at once but some brimmed over, and she jumped up and went away to the bottom of the garden. Was it anything you said to her? Tell me, and I'll tease her.

Austin repeated every word of Susan's little story again and again. He pictured the two girls sitting near each other, Susan watching and laughing at the wagtail and forgetting Faith awhile, turning round then suddenly and meeting that face with the "spilling tears." The lips on the brink of trembling; the pale sweet patient face, and the spilling tears; he felt a singular felicity in this and returned again and again to the picture. He sighed deeply but felt happy.

Practising, he said she always used to finish her practice in the morning, and come out at this hour. Well, well, what an incredible fool I am of late. The "Transcendental Schema!"—And I spent the time dreaming on a schoolgirl's moods, tut. But only a few days more. He softened.

She is a sweet little girl, I wish I had her for a sister. Then I would like her very well without troubling. . . . The spilling tears.

Faith had come down into the garden thinking he had gone. She did not notice him until she was close and then turned suddenly to steal back unobserved. He bounded to her side and took her hands and laughed as she hung her head.

You wept, Faith, you wept. Susan told me all about it. It was very sweet to hear that you wept.

He tried to look her in the face, but springing aside quickly she escaped into the house.

Faith was at practice and fulfilling that task very dutifully as he entered the room next morning. She looked up a little nervously and beheld him looking at her attentively.

Excuse me, Faith, I have not come to interrupt you but—a walk this afternoon, Faith?

Yes.

He caught her hand quickly and kissed and with a quick warm pressure let it go. A stream of cordial influence flowed in with the clasp. Faith's practice had not suffered interruption, and he left the room at once.

They walked a long distance in silence that afternoon, but this silence was a happy thing.

Why did you walk in the gutter and over tufts of grass, Faith? he inquired. So as to be at least half the width of the road away from me.

Well, and Faith pouted, I don't know. It isn't fair, Austin; you think you can play with me because I am only a schoolgirl yet —You laughed at my lessons and you questioned—and—you never tell me anything.

He looked at her somewhat amused.

Let me see your palm, that's what the gipsies ask, you know.

She took off her glove. He kissed the hand quickly and then held it in his own.

You're an interesting little being, Faith, and now I do feel half inclined to tell you something.

Some of my earliest recollections, Faith, are about this very place where we are walking now. I can remember as a child, here one beautiful spring morning. The rain had fallen with a light shower and now the sun had come out from behind a cloud. The air was deliciously cool and free. My heart beat high and with my walk breaking into a sort of skip or dance, that kept time to the rising of my spirit, I sang to myself a kind of chant. I can see now the light spray as it sparkled from the springing of a twig, I can feel the touch of the water drops as I struck them from the leaves as I passed, and the monotonous chant was telling me of deeds that I should do; the pictures stood clear. The pure air was fresh to drink, and my spirit leapt lightly, and the blue sky and the golden colouring of the sun were in my pictures too. You look up, Faith. I too with not less unexplained wonder.

I would be a soldier. Night and day the thought was ever with me. It haunted me, and as I grew, became my natural way of thinking. I never doubted. I never questioned.

That madness of a child had consequences that tell on me now. It saved me from death.—

From death, Austin!

Yes. By discipline, training, and the exercise I indulged in under the care of Alec. Church. Perhaps the only person I ever envied or can envy in the world was Alec. Church.

Who? Alec. Church!

Yes. We were about the same age and as youngsters played together. Alec. wanted to be a soldier too. He was a stout urchin and I thought him a Pollux. Even now he could pose for a Dancing Fawn.

The design of a military life, its glory, seems to me now a gruesome farce. In silence it had grown up within me, and in silence I saw it fade in the sober light of day, and felt the fearful void. More than half the battle of life I believe is to throw one's self into the proper groove. The dull man, and the able man, it carries on and forms their characters. Not one man in a thousand, in politics, or business, or even in intellectual matters, can raise himself above his groove; not one man in a million bases his life, projects it forth, guides it upon deeply thought-out principles. Fetiches have been the lure of heroes; bubbles have flung nations into slaughter; the bubbles that mere mad currents have flung into my life are swelled up to things of worship by men.

My engineering course held on. It had lost its impulse and a higher one I had not seen as yet. The care of building up a constitution brought me into athletic company. I pursued that with a fiery zeal.

H'm. It was a fine idea that of the ancient Greeks, Faith, that το καλον.

Faith looked up in surprise.

It means "The Beautiful," Faith. Mind and body trained in harmony—Aristotle sets it forth: The mind, great in thought and feeling; the body supple, graceful, strong. Sophocles danced at the head of the procession of youths, and each movement and the pose of sculptured limbs was informed with meaning from the poet's mind. The fragments of Phidias have the dignity of demigods.

Well, why it is so not now to explore, but, simply, my own experiences made me familiar with minds as coarse as they were feeble. The row up the river was followed by beer out of pewters at the Waterman's Arms. Athletic company meant athletic talk. I became an authority on running, racing, and prize-fighting. Well do I remember the look in Standard Bearer's eyes as he came out to win the Derby and how I bent to catch the movement of his swinging stride. You never heard of Standard Bearer, perhaps?

No.

He was a hero of the turf! Why, Faith, there is a boundless literature there, and men whom the world has delighted to honour have devoted their lives to the sport. At athletic meetings at this time when all were jolly, I often also drank too much.

But Faith! . . . Cards and billiards were like an article of religion.

Austin!

Austin meditated a moment. . . . It seemed incredible, the fev'rous passions that had eaten into his life.

* * * * *

My eyes were always hungry for a brighter glimpse. Gradually I separated. My nature bore me further off until I stood aloof.

You seem, Austin, always to have lived two lives.

Yes, until the lower, all that I was known for, seemed almost to have swallowed up the other. Hateful enough now it seems to me, —but I can see, too, more clearly now than then, how mortally difficult that separation was. Habits formed, soul callous, resolution lax, ideas steeped in the atmosphere we breathe, obligations, too, kind hearts, familiar bands, the ties of sacrifices.

* * * * *

Well the stork wades in water, the owl flits in the dusk. The instrument to its work. My fields were far away. I knew men of every stamp, men absorbed in their ambitions, but their way was not mine.

I was alone, without an aim, without a creed, with no bright surroundings here, filled with desperate denials, and with a fever fretting at my life.

* * * * *

I worked wildly at times. My mind, continually pressed on, ranged in this field and that voraciously. My toils were long, severe, but I was restless, plied and harassed everywhere, with no reward. I fell into fits of illness and again the gradual steps brought me to look on death. . . . Has this any interest for you, Faith?

Yes, Austin, said Faith with some earnestness, tell it to me right through. I think I see on every side more than you have cared to say.

He walked a long time in silence and inwardly blessed the sweet being by his side.

Well. I cannot go into metaphysics just now, Faith, to make it clear how I reasoned out my changes. Illness brought patience. It made me see things calmly. I still felt a spirit quenchless and my old ambition was beginning to sing new songs. The rapture of the strife was there. The mutual play of mind on mind delighted me.

I saw at once a larger scope in politics, a field more varied, delightful. I read good works, and exercised my thoughts very patiently, and felt great desires to do something for our native land. I formed a plan; that was law. But, for one thing, I lacked the means to carry it on, and, wretched me, became a pedagogue.

* * * * *

While at school I used to practise elocution on the sea beach away in a secluded spot. I had learnt many of the best passages off by heart and used to give them forth.

Ever task on task, Austin.

No, no. That never was a task. But often, when tired in mind and body, I used to drag myself to the familiar spot; and there with the fresh cool breeze, and with the thoughts these poems brought, my weariness would fall as from off my shoulders like a load.

My solitary rambles are grateful recollections. My mind was then exalted, my heart was pure. My enthusiasm for politics was gradually cooled —

But why?

In a hundred curious ways, Faith. Even you, practical, decided, little person, he said laughing, will admit, that a condition for success is to convince others of one's utility. I read, observed, applied myself to think, to work, to hold the scales impartially. That was already fatal to any hopes with a party. Soon I was removed from the limits of all parties. Suffice it, no constituency would have elected me if I had been Apollo. That was practical. With politics would fall my law. I would be once more without a goal distinct. I had worked hard and had gained husks. I had endured the drudgery, reached no reward. One cheers one's way with hopes and promised harvest. Vanity, ambition, fill the mind with pictures. I had vanities enough and foolish ambitions, but I saw my pictures fading. However, I was a free man,—no party, no sect, no —

Faith's head had been bent in deep thought.

If it was right to do, Austin, she said, it was right to do.

Austin had been speaking as though speaking to himself.

Faith, he said, you said you did not care for poetry. Tell me how you like this.

Music yearning like a God in pain.

. . . . . .

APPROACHES. 57

Music that comes swooning over hollow ground

. . . . . .

Rain scented eglantine gave temperate sweets to that well-wooing sun.

Or these in another strain?

To bear all naked truths,
And to envisage circumstance, all calm,
That is the top of Sovereignty.

Or this?

Are then regalities all gilded masks?
No. There are throned seats unscalable
But by a patient wing, a constant spell—

Well then, let me finish or shall we talk about Spencer and the Principles of Evolution?

Go on.

Nay, but Faith, it is excellent good if you would but think on it as this man hath set it down. Your caterpillar, forsooth, works assiduously for his caterpillar state, but Nature had said—Thou shall be a butterfly—

Well Austin? Tell me why you gave up the law, even then.

Because my only interest in it was as a

stepping stone to public life. The daily practice of a barrister's profession I abhorred. I believe about this time it was I first had moral courage.

I had always heard you praised for that.

No. I think I see my way clearer now, Faith.

* * * * *

Truth is the innermost spirit of all that is sacred. Science binds us to Nature, grasps her powers, informs the way. O that this had come to me years ago when my mind was livelier to that indelible impress, my spirit unimpaired.

Faith smiled.

Faith, I have poured out the precious wine of life into the sordid earth. The wicked who flourish like the bay tree would drain my blood. If I were to die now I would be a figment. But that will not be, I hope. My life of experience has been a narrow one, and a shallow one. This possibly has made my feeling deeper for what I love. The worst I have braced myself up for—to leave my home, and now, you.

They walked along in silence, but he clasped her hand tightly.

Tired? Sweet Faith. Tired, grave little heroine? he asked.

No, Austin.

Yet we have walked on hour after hour.

I have not noticed. I did not think of it and—no, Austin, I do not feel tired at all.

Faith, I must soon lose the sight of you, and for years we will not see each other more. How precious seem now these fleeting hours. The picture that always comes to me, Faith, is of the first time I saw you, doing your arithmetic. I remember the seat you had, the dress you wore, the lamp, the little pale patient face, Faith, as it looked up to mine. And now, Faith, these next few years will make more difference to you than all the years that you have lived before. You will find a world that you can scarcely picture now, a fuller world, a deeper world, and in that world trials too that happily you know not of. It is all the change from girlhood to womanhood.

He stopped, and Faith's head was bent.

Faith, you are a sweet good girl. I know that you will be a sweet and good woman.

His voice was firm—to Faith's ears the words throbbed out.

He raised her hand to his lips and the kiss he pressed on it was the purest he had known. Faith went straight to her room when they reached home, and locked the door and remained long sitting on her bed. Her face was filled with an earnest look. Then she knelt down beside her bed and in the stillness prayed. The next morning Faith was late for breakfast. The little maiden's heart was full.

Late scholar, cried Susan.

Austin looked up hastily. The face was warm and rosy generally. The lids were fine beneath the eyes. She looked pale now and the lids were swollen.

Austin rose and placed a chair for her between himself and Susan, and in doing so pressed her hand. Susan noticed that.

You should have been in time to pour out my tea, little girl he said, but now I will pour out yours instead.

Faith, will you play a brief half-hour for me to-night, alone. Play the pieces I like and once for me alone, sweet Faith.

Yes, Austin I will do that.

And Faith—

Well.

We'll go for a walk this afternoon. Say, yes. But, Faith, the last day I will be here. The last day it seems strange to say it, seems hard to say now that it has come, but long afterwards it will seem stranger and harder to have said it. Well, Faith, we will after tea, for the sun sets late, take a walk together up the hill. How many a time have we stood there together even in the years gone by. It is a beautiful day and the sunset will be beautiful. That too will be something to remember. This once, Faith, to have had a last look. Then a brief half-hour of the music and then you are free.

Yes, Austin, let us all go together. There are others whom—

I know. That is taken for granted. I have the whole day and the evening for them. I go away very early in the morning, and have made them all promise not to get up to see me off, so we will sit up talking late and say good-bye to night. . . . Ah! Faith. It is something above me that has led my life. I cannot stay. I cannot stay. I have not lived. A dungeon wall is closing over me. It is like the depths beneath the face of day, beneath the earth and its life, where one sees now the stars only. It is a dream. I struggle. A chariot, whirling, shaken, doubtful, has suspended a moment its course, I leap on the car.

He walked with Susan with his arm round her waist, and her little girlish history they talked out. With Harold he played like a schoolboy, and the youngster came then and sat on his knee, realizing that he was going away, and threw his arms about his neck.

*　　*　　*　　*　　*

This tastes sweetly to me, Faith, this air of my birth-place and fills my lungs as no other. And now we have reached the hill top. Let me take this memory away. It will come again how often. And sweeter than all, to remember you here. If you were a fairy, Faith, and could see my way, would you whisper to me when you saw me stumbling and forfend the evil from me?

Austin, your own character ought to be strong enough.

And if you had a talisman, so that when I were in danger it might save me, if I were falling would set my feet straight, and in the dark night with its light guide my way, would you give it?

You know I do not understand you, Austin. I have no *soul*, she said and smiled.

He laughed. Well then, Faith, behold. It is not only in fairy tales that mortals are defended by the grace of higher powers. Soon now I go to unknown regions, beyond thy fair dominion, Faith. Will you kiss me, sweetheart?

No, Austin.

And why not, Faith, if your kiss could do me good.

No. It is not right.

Nevertheless, Faith, will you not give me a kiss?

Austin, you know it is not right.

But right to me perhaps?

No, I think not.

Then why not that much?—O how soon you will have forgotten me—a look perchance at the little book I gave you, and say, Ah yes, I remember, it was Austin gave me that.

I do not require that to remember you by, Austin. But listen. Before I came here on this visit I thought I knew you well. Now I see I knew nothing of you. I had formed a good opinion of you—

Well!

Now—I scarcely know how to say it. Austin, I will try to explain. I now see that your true character I had never struck upon. It is, yes, you can be incredibly—foolish.

Austin smiled.

Then again. I—had—never—seen—you—touched before.

Go on!

And—and I feel glad you are going away—

I mean for your sake! Austin. You

think, no doubt, that there is something devastating, as you call it, in discussing your plans with those that cannot understand you.

Don't talk rubbish!

Well, then, it is hard to be to persons not what you really seem, and many a time when you play with their frivolity it has a bad effect upon yourself. I have noticed that.

You have been observant, little girl.

You have not treated me properly.

You! What! How so?

For one thing you laughed at my studies without telling me the reason. Yes, I understood—you're being splendidly schooled, Faith! That I didn't mind so much because I used to think myself at times that they were rather dreary. But you also seemed to laugh—at me, as one might at a—at a child!

Austin laughed outright.

Good! Faith.

Well, Austin, it was really too bad. And then you wished me to write to you. You would for all that criticize my letters as if I

were a master of arts and laugh at them too.
And then, it is nothing to squeeze the hand
of a little girl, to call her—*sweetheart*, and
yet in talking to me you seemed often
enough to forget that I was but a schoolgirl
yet. And then you wanted me to—that is
you said—*kiss me*.

Austin smiled.

Oh, it is not right, Austin. And how soon
would I be remembered as a silly little fool.
How soon will you forget me altogether now,
where you will meet others too in everything
superior to me.

No, little executioner, that will not be
the case. But you are right. I have
thought of it as you spoke. It would not
be right, even to ask you to kiss me. You
are still a little girl and have your experience
before you. I think I could still smile to
see you happy, Faith—when I returned—if
you were really happy, bearing another
name.

You speak coolly!

Yes, Faith, but not entirely because I have
no feeling.

Austin, are you angry? It was bold of me to speak —

Angry! with you? But let us look round, Faith, one last look, before we go.

From the hill they looked down upon the sleepy little town, and then across the stream to Austin's home. Quiet and sequestered, the row of trees behind the garden, the house half hid, the slowly ascending smoke, the mother and Susan and Harold, they could see—it was a picture of peace. They turned from this to look upon the setting sun. The low ridge of hills looked blue in the distance, the sun sinking gradually was disappearing now, and over the irregularly waving lines of the ridge projecting in the sky seemed to run a mighty stream of molten gold, and above floated and through impenetrable depths receded a field of crimson light; and then above again more sombre masses skirted with purple, and flecked and dappled with lighter hues, beginning to deepen into evening's shade. It was a hushed time. The two stood together hand in hand; the sun had set, and he drew her hand tighter and raised it to his lips.

Now once, Austin, before we go down let me look at you upon this hill, and this will be the image I will try to hold.

He bent his head.

No. You'll find afterwards that this study will begin to fade, and the impression you will remember will be one that has come on quickly perhaps and unawares. But, Faith, you are very sweet to me. You have nestled in my very heart, and now have become a part of me. I cannot let you go. You are the dearest of all, my little darling, and you will be, little woman, my sweet wife. I must say it. You will be a woman when I see you again —

Austin, recollect! You have no right so to speak. It is not fair—to me. Let us forget this,—and we will go down at once and have the music now—and then will part good friends and both hopeful of the future.

He caught her in his arm and tried to draw her to him.

She swerved away, with head bent low,

and as he held her by the waist, her hand was put up and turned away to him, as though to protect her face. He could not forbear a smile.

Come then, Faith, let's go down, and Faith blushing in her sweet serious way gave him her hand, and they descended the hill together.

Now a half-hour of the music, and I will bear away this load.

They passed into the room and Faith played the simple pieces he could understand and finished with Auld Robin Gray.

She stopped and he remained silent.

Through all its pathos, he felt a sombre sense of shame that he had ever broached a deep matter with her.

She came and sat beside him on the sofa. Her cheeks were warm. And Austin—she had come to him and sat beside him and given him her hand—a warm and undulating tide flowed over him.

He took up a little book from the table.

And this is my keepsake to you. It is the least costly of all my books for I paid sixpence for it, but I like this man, Walt Whitman.

Austin, this is more precious to you than to me. You know I have no *soul!* Why do you smile? I will not even promise to read it, Austin.

Nay, then, but if I say, because I gave it, will you keep it?

Yes, Austin.

He read the " Prayer of Columbus " in a deep voice.

* * * * *

O I am sure they really came from thee,
The urge, the ardour, the unconquerable will,
The potent, felt, interior command, stronger than words,
A message from the Heavens whispering to me even in
    sleep,
These sped me on.

* * * * *

Yes, Austin, I like that.

Then opening the book, he held it for her to read and they both looked into it together.

* * * * *

Among the men and women the multitude
I perceive one picking me out by secret and divine signs
Acknowledging none else, not parent, wife, husband,
    brother, child, any nearer than I am,

APPROACHES. 71

Some are baffled but that one is not—that one knows me.
Ah lover and perfect equal,
I meant that you should discover me so by faint indirections
And I when I meet you mean to discover you by the like in you.

. . . . . .

Whoever you are, now I place my hand upon you, that you be my poem,
I whisper with my lips close to your ear,
I have loved many women and men, but I love none better than you.

. . . . . .

O you whom I often and silently come where you are that I may be with you,
As I walk by your side, or sit near, or remain in the same room with you,
Little you know the subtle electric fire that for your sake is playing within me.

* * * * *

He watched her face and saw the earnestness deepen there as her eyes still looked upon the book. He placed his arm round her waist and laid his head a moment on her breast. He could hear the heart racing. He looked up again and she was still gazing resolutely at the book, and he saw the desperate effort of control, though her chest began to rise and fall.

Faith, my sweetheart, my sweetheart, this half-hour is the dearest of my life, and you will —

Austin! cried Susan running into the room, where have you been? We've been looking everywhere for you.

They spent the evening together — and after their simple partings, Susan bore Faith off with an expression of much hopefulness, and left Austin and his mother alone, for the last.

He lay down for a couple of hours—the early morning was cold and dreary when he rose. While he dressed, his movements he noticed himself had a peculiar air of quietness and method.

And now in the fresh breeze his spirits rose. He harnessed his horse to drive into Gresham, and the last few minutes were at hand. He was hesitating whether to return to the house or not, when he saw Nora standing at the kitchen door and beckoning him.

Well—well, Nora, did I not say how angry I would be if anyone got up to see me off?

Nora laughed.

See here I've made you some nice warm cocoa in this little jug, and with this nice toast and these eggs, and this gingerbread I made last night, you'll do till you get to Gresham.

Nora!

Austin laughed. Come then we'll have breakfast together. Do you not feel cold, getting up so early?

Cold. No, I can get up at any hour in my —, that is without dressing, and not feel cold.

By Jupiter, you're a splendid girl! cried Austin with admiration undisguised. We have a nation before us, Nora. Pat too is a splendid fellow, isn't he?

Oh, he'll do. He's right enough in his way. And—Well he's something to look at, and that's more than every girl can say.

He is. There's a nation before us, Nora! You will pull along grandly together, but, Nora,—make him *lieutenant* on the wedding-day.

Nora laughed.

Oh, I'll manage him finely, and—she came and whispered in Austin's ear, I've saved over a hundred and fifty pounds and put it in the bank for all the time I've been here.

Good, good, good! Nora. And you never told me a word of that before—thought I might tell Pat! Oh, no, that wouldn't do. But Nora run down and bring up my horse, and I'll be ready when you come.

He passed Faith's door. It was a little open—a wild light came into his eyes. His heart throbbed and struggled. What restrained —

I must see her—I must see her once again.

The day was dawning and, through the curtains, shadowed in the room. The room was small and with the simplest furniture, but there was an aspect that struck him with a new appreciation. He gazed upon the sleeping girl and his mind was chastened.

How pure, how sweet she was. The pale patient face was still and calm, the sleep had Nature's blessing, the sweet sleep of health and innocence. His breath was hushed as he looked down at her. He knelt by the bedside, with unformed thought, and almost inarticulate form of speech, breathed forth God bless her—God bless her, and bent forward and touched her forehead with his lips.

The eyelids faintly quivered. The fair skin seemed softly tinged. The arm was moved a little, the lips disparted, a pulse of life had come into the form.

He bent again and with his lips touched hers, and glided from the room.

Nora pressed and kissed his hand before he drove away, and wept till he was out of sight, and dried her eyes upon her white apron, and went back to her room again.

Austin's face was turned now towards a pilgrimage. His eye shone clearly, and if something of sadness still so serene it might have been a smile that played about his lips.

CHAPTER V.

Months rolled on—

Faith's little day at home was now filled up with music, household duties, reading, walking in the fields, meditation.

Her thoughts to be sure wandered and struggled at times. She felt her spirit—and the gradual discovery filled her mind at first with something of a maidenly restraint—too active, too resolute, not to know the intimations of her future wider life.

The present was cheerful enough in its monotony. She had love about her, her mind was nurtured healthily. The past— there was a sort of wistfulness in that. Yet she looked back to the past oftener, truly, than she gave herself permission.

So the months slipped by unnoticeable for anything but the growth of mind, and body, their wholesome prospering. A sweet life, doubtless, yet even Faith was not wholly happy.

They were sitting together one evening after tea, Faith and her mother. The evening was mild, and now, in the summer, long, so that they had not drawn the curtains yet. The sun had set; they had remained silent. Where were Faith's thoughts?

She possibly would not have told. There was a sunset in the picture that she formed. Yet Faith was not a sentimental girl, we think. The patience of her cheek was matched by resolution in the eyes; more that than pensive.

Mama, she said now, we have been together so long—I wonder what you would ever do without me. You would miss me very much?

Yes, Faith—but you have some reason for asking now? and she took her daughter's hand. I know, Faith, though you never say a word, how dull must be your life here, sometimes, and you are no longer a little girl now —

No, mama, it is not that—it is not that I feel myself dull here—but—

Well? Faith, you would make some proposal. It is only right too that you should have a chance. You would like to go to Dudley again, to carry on your education, and your music.—Well, Faith, what is it?

Well then I would like to study medicine.

Good gracious, child! what has put that notion into your head so suddenly?

It is not suddenly, mama. I have been thinking over it for a long time. At first I was afraid to form such a plan myself, but then—at length I got accustomed to thinking of it—as right—then I was afraid to say anything about it to you, for fear you would not understand me.—No, I don't mean that exactly—in case you should think it not called for. I practise my music here, and study, and read one book after another here, but do not seem to myself to—to come any further —to know anything really. Then—do you not think a woman ought to be—I don't know how to say it—independent?

Mrs. Shenstone looked at the little woman sitting on the low stool beside her, and though somewhat struck by these ideas could not repress a smile.

Well, perhaps, Faith. You don't wish to be so easily besieged and left without defences, eh? she said laughing.

Don't be silly, mama, said Faith hiding her surprised wild blush, you silly little, little mama. I think it's I that have the sense after all.

They both laughed now.

Very well then, my little Zenobia, but help me to clear away the tea things now, for doubtless it is growing dark.

Time wore on, and Faith kept her purpose, and by becoming familiar with it, and hearing Faith's arguments, and after consulting her sister-in-law, Mrs. Shenstone arranged that Faith should go to the University and there work out her education. Her aunt, an excellent lady whose only daughter had recently been married, and gone to other lands, invited Faith to live with her.

Faith too resumed with great pleasure her acquaintance with Mrs. Neville and her little daughter, Mary. Her studies occupied much of her time; she and Mrs. Neville often played music together; and in the afternoons putting on her bonnet, for they lived in a little country suburb, Faith and Mary would often go for a ramble in the fields.

She knew few people and never seemed to wish more, and between her and the little girl a peculiar tender friendship grew.

Mary must have been about ten years old then, but tall for her age. Her figure was slight, but her carriage full of spirit. An ambitious little figure, Faith said. The little girl had an abundance of a sort of auburn hair, fine skin, and the delicate lines about the mouth, and the delicately moulded features, moved in a thousand changes and shades—the dainty peeping half-discovered thoughts with all their witchery to charm. Violet might have been the colour of her eyes, you could not guess as they looked at you. People would stare surprised involuntarily upon those orbs, and never know. It was a face of peculiar beauty. Animated usually the features were, but even in the midst of this would come a look—something of wondering in its unconscious earnestness, not grave, too luminous it seemed, not sad either, though it gave something of these feelings to her who loved her best.

Mary had never been to school yet, but had learnt to read so long ago that she could not recollect beginning, and in this direction only had her education been much fostered. Of books she had read an astonishing number, not all such as a child would usually select, and to Faith she was accustomed to relate fairy tales that her own fancy conjured up.

In other matters she was a remarkably ignorant little girl and Faith in her practical way urged that she should be sent to school.

Delicate! I can never understand your always saying that, said Faith in reply to Mrs. Neville's objections. Look at her eyes how bright they are, and how active she is. We walk about and play about by the hour, and she very seldom tires. Or if she rests for a little while she seems to be all animation soon again. She's very thin, but then she has grown so fast. I think she would be better if she had some nice companions of her own age to play with, instead of reading so much and imagining those extraordinary fairy tales of hers.

Mrs. Neville shook her head.

No, no, she said. Mary is like no one else. Her reading has not done her harm. It is her great delight, it would be wrong to rob her of it. If she went to school—No, that routine of lessons and tasks and learning by rote. No, Faith. What you have said to me would be true for any little girl I have seen but Mary. I would send her too if she were strong, but her temperament is a peculiar one. Poor little thing—she stopped and to Faith's surprise, who could not understand it, sighed.

Mrs. Neville had in these years greatly altered—the features, the figure too, the carriage. Her hair was streaked with grey, her face was pale, looked too at first glance sad. Her eyes had lost their flashing lights. Her manner was cheerful but composed.

It was a face that grew on one.

There was in it that that gave to others sympathy and drew from them their confidence. There was strength too in that gentle face, and a beauty of a finer type than she had worn before.

I have observed Mary almost anxiously, she said again, she is all spirit, and although no occasion has come before you to notice it, hurtfully, painfully, sensitive. No,—no, I will not send her to school.

I confess, said Faith with a smile, you really do not convince me. She is so sensitive as you say, because she has never had companions of her own age. But where is she now?

She is in her room sleeping—came in looking quite weary with the heat, and I made her take her shoes off and rest a little.

The door opened and in came Mary, running in dressed in a white dress with her long hair floating over her shoulders. Her eyes were sparkling as with merriment. What eyes she had!

Faith looked up in triumph as she came.

Mary delicate—no more than I am, she said to herself, though to be sure Faith was no Amazon.

Come here, Mary, cried both in the same breath.

Mary looked from one to the other.

You've been talking about me and Mama has been saying nasty things about me! I heard her once telling your Auntie, Faith, that I was—Am I not very strong, Faith? Nearly as strong as you, Eh?

Yes, to be sure, Mary, come and sit on my knee.

Yes, I will, Mama, I will go to Faith now. Little grave face, Faith looks quite a little woman, said she, peering critically into her face. I do declare she looks as serious and tries to look as sensible as quite a little woman. Pretends to be motherly to me when we go out for a walk.—Now, Mary, don't wet your feet there! Poor little Faith with her motherly cares.

She laughed and threw her arms about Faith's neck and kissed her.

It is too bad to have so many mothers as I've got. If I have the least thing wrong with me, Mama frets herself out as much as if—as if I were really ill. If I stir at night she rises to see if I want anything. I believe she must lie awake all night, and she seems a little disappointed, or at least she asks me a lot of times to be sure, if I say I am quite well. Foolish Mama. If I cut my finger I have to keep it to myself for fear she'll want to bandage it, she laughed. Isn't it too bad, Faith?

Yes, Mary, of course it is; you are a famous little girl and will be a regular—who was that pedestrianizing young lady in the old Greek mythology?

Pedestrianizing?—Oh you mean Atalanta —running after the golden apples, eh?

Mary certainly was not delicate, Faith was sure of that. She laughed, and played, and teased, and climbed about Faith, and talked away at a great rate and kissed her with much energy. Then she ran and jumped into her mother's lap.

And what do you think of going to school? said Faith as they walked their fragrant path.

I really don't know, Faith, replied the little girl with an air of meditation. Sometimes I think it would be nice. I know I ought to learn something some day, but I think I like reading better than lessons. Of course I would like to be very wise and very grave! like little Faith is, said she looking up at her archly, but that comes on very gradually! How did you like school, eh?

Oh, very well, said Faith, you meet little girls of your own age to play with. You soon find someone you like very well, and then you're happy. I had Edith Howard and we were great friends. We used to bring our lunch to school because it was too far to go home, and we used sometimes in the winter to make toast by the fire and drink our cocoa and tell stories in the dinner hour. It was great fun. Fairy tales weren't so bad then, but your foolish little noodle is always running on them.

Edith Howard, tell me all about her said Mary opening her eyes with interest already. Fair or dark?

Rather dark.

Tall or short?

Medium, a little dumpy, perhaps.

H'm, and Mary tried to form a pleasant picture on this basis. Not dumpy though, Faith? She could be small, you know, without being dumpy.

But she was dumpy! with a nose a little turned up, and not a bit good-looking; she was one of the cleverest girls at the school though, and what's better one of the nicest too.

Very well, said Mary, she'll do for every day. Now tell me about some others.

Let me see. O, yes. There was May Anderson, a little girl with fair hair and the bluest of eyes, and the winsomest little ways in the world. Poor little May, you couldn't help loving her.

Fair hair and blue eyes and winsome manner, this promised better; and Mary pictured her with her long hair flowing loosely over her shoulders and with a slender staff with a star or something of the kind on top; and then she asked all sorts of questions about her.

And is she living now? she inquired anxiously.

Of course, you might meet her some day.

Mary opened her eyes very wide indeed at this.

Her parents were not well off and she went as a governess to a family in Gresham.

A governess! but people always treat them badly—as if they were nobody in the world—

You're bringing your reading into play now, eh? It's not aways so bad though— for there are many good people in the world.

Mary hoped sincerely that she would be very happy and began sketching out a husband who was young, and very handsome and at first very unfortunate, even sad, she went so far, but who latterly had attained a fairy-like resource of doing by unexpected strokes the most wonderful good things. She heaved a sigh as she left her well provided and questioned Faith again.

Well then there was Rosy Beamish. She was really a good girl, though a very human being, Mary. She had a round good-natured face and long brown hair, a little girl, but with the daintiest little figure—like—you know the picture of the dancing girl we were looking at.

Good, good.

With nice soft brown eyes, and when she opened them on you, little shadows seemed to be in the corners with little twinkles peeping out.

Rosy was the great peace-maker, because everybody liked her and she seemed always to understand both sides. Rosy—yes, she was a really good girl. I don't believe anyone was fonder of play than she was, but she thought she would have to be a governess too, or something of the sort, and she used to work at her lessons like a little tiger, and if she was set down a place in class we could see it at once in her—poor little Ro—

But she was nearly always top.

And what became of her? Did she have to be a governess? No.

For a little while she taught at the same school herself; just lately she is married, I see—

Married, to whom?

Her husband is an Engineer, and his name I saw was Robert MacLaren, and I don't know anything more about him; will that satisfy you? But I hope they will be happy enough.

Mary sincerely hoped so too. She had formed some picture of an unfortunate young prince or at least an exile for Rosy—and it is a little hard at times to come down to the reality.

These and a hundred other things they talked about made Mary wish to go to school and learn to know friends too.

The lessons, Faith assured her, she would not mind so much, and some she would like when once she had got into the habit of

doing them always at the same time.
Further her reading would help her, she
would soon get on.

Mary had a narrow escape the day she
persuaded Ethel James to allow her to mount
her pony. It bolted and "flew along," so
Mary said, the footpath in the park. Faith
beheld her coming, Mary crouching down and
clinging to the saddle with both hands, the
bridle trailing on the ground. The workmen
returning from their work simply frightened
the beast the more, but Mary was "the
frightender" she said. Faith sprang and
caught the bridle with some wild hope of
clinging to a tree. She was flung down and
trailed along; the pony checked, reared, and
plunged under a stretching bough. Mary
desperately caught hold and let her palfrey
go, the bough broke and Mary fell. Faith
with her heart throbbing, her ears humming,
with half-blinded eyes, saw Mary rise to her
feet, stand head bent a moment; then
pursing her lips the little girl dashed her
closed hand across her forehead as though
brushing something aside, and flung herself

erect. Bruised and beaten, as she was herself, Faith smiled as she looked, but there was something that made her knit her brows as though a faint remembrance had come and vanished then. They agreed "not to tell Mama."

I came a cropper though, said Mary ruefully.

What! Slang, Mary?

Yes, I know, but I saw it in a book once, and it seemed just now to fit.

Faith smiled at Mary's rueful look through which her laughing dimples were even peeping now.

Very well then, Mary, you're a good little crock.

What! Slang, Faith?

Yes, I know, said Faith, but I saw it in a book once—and it seemed just now to fit.

They laughed, and Faith took her in her arms, and stooped to kiss her. Mary offered her lips and then drew aside and looked up archly at Faith.

What! cried Faith, another of your unending little tricks, is it? You want to be begged for your kisses, or to be won for them, little girl.

I scarcely know whether to admire you or not, said Mary, leaping like a tiger at horses, and—

I did not do it for admiration, cried Faith, but truly for your own sweet self.

She pressed her to her breast, and now tightly as she had seen the mother do, and placed her cheek beside hers. Mary's great eyes were swimming as she pressed her lips to Faith's, and Faith smothered her in kisses.

Mrs. Neville had given way to Faith's arguments and to Mary's own wish at last. She gravely told her Mama, with the air somewhat of a stoic, that she was really getting now too old for fairy tales; and so, taut and trim, little Mary was launched in the ocean of life as it seemed to her. She dropped into school ways and betook herself to school lessons in a way that surprised Faith, but not her mother. All her little wilful ways, her capful of caprices, her playful surprises, were put now under discipline. She learnt rapidly, as they had all expected, and as she felt her ignorance dreadfully—she confided in Faith—began to set about her tasks with zeal.

She seemed transformed at once from a wild and wanton little creature, with her wallet of old fairy tales, to a neatly tucked-up schoolgirl, with all decorous incidents, habits methodical, good conduct cards, and R on her "sums" to come home with.

Still Mary was not made of gingerbread; in fact, she behaved like a little fiend once at school. They were at prayers it seemed, and Mary had peeped up. Miss Mawe was watching "with the side of her eye."

Miss Mawe was very snappy on that particular day, and declared that Mary had put out her tongue. Mary stood up.

You *know* I would not do it, she afterwards told Faith in relating the event.

Mary was dreadfully hurt.

You ought to be ashamed and humiliated, cried Mrs. Mawe, and I will punish you well. Stay in after school and do 100 lines of poetry for me to-night.

You—can—do—them—your—self! said

Mary. This was audacity out of all bounds. What!

Miss Mawe raised her hand, but the face was too beautiful with the deep wonderful eyes.

Mary, standing like a seraph, put up her hands to her head, and slowly, deliberately, pulled out the beautiful hair, and shewed it —long streamers in her hand—and still looking up at Miss Mawe walked backwards out to the door.

But this was only once, and things might have gone well, but the mother was right after all. The little being's cheek began to pale, except when excited, as with her reading, then it used to flush. Faith would like to have seen again at times the arch look, the dimples, the arbitrary little tyrannies of hers—not always that " quiet good little girl." The earnest look that Mrs. Neville had seemed to see oftener than anybody else, Faith began now to observe.

Mary made no complaint; she did not seem to have any to make. She praised the school, took interest in her lessons, had some companions she was very fond of, liked all the others, and thought the teachers very good and very kind. Poor little girl; who, meeting those deep earnest eyes looking up, where a spirit seemed to live whose motions knew love only, could have cherished feelings that did not issue too in love?

Poor little girl; they used to smile as they marked her unconscious peculiar airs of some superiority, it seemed.

Nevertheless she was not looking well now, and Faith was agreed she ought to have a holiday. She caught a sore throat on the first day of her holiday, and it was only a patient, feeble, little Mary that rose from her bed again, not at all the arbitrary little being with her laughter, and her wiles, that used to play about the house.

Faith's examination now occupied her time. She had prepared for it carefully. Her only relaxation had been the company of her aunt, her conversations, and her music, her walks with Mrs. Neville and Mary, or as usual in the afternoon, with the little girl alone.

When she looked back the year seemed to have flown by.

It was a season of good thoughts, and these were treasured now in the recollections that came upon her mind. She was successful.

Poor little Mary, for the child's sake, she had spoken full of cheer; truth to say she was getting well again almost as rapidly it seemed as she had fallen ill. Faith's heart was full as she returned once more to her home.

THE COMING HOME.

CHAPTER VI.

THE good ship *India* was rolling slowly from side to side in the long swell of the dark green waves. The end of the voyage was approaching. The weather had been favourable, and this day was very fine, with the blue sky overhead.

Austin had been sitting reading, casting his eyes now and then on the coast of a distant island, where the long swell was broken. A breaker would show white, seem to run a moment under the overhanging cliff, then disappear. The white surf would show itself then further on as though leaping out of the bosom of the sea, then sink back into nothingness for ever. Bleak and deserted the island was—a dangerous coast for the ships, and they gave it a wide berth, there in its solitariness,—the play of the waters, the crisp tossing of the billows into sea spray, then the sinking into the dark waves below, the white foam that appeared and was carried curling round the cliffs' edge, then disappeared for ever—so for ages round this desolate shore, unseen by human eyes, the waves have played; so for the ages that will follow our brief span of life, when all our records are dim figments of the past, the breaking water there will rise, show white, and disappear.

Austin rose and paced the quarter deck. In the years that had elapsed he had become profoundly learned, or at least the passengers on board had so assured themselves. He had that morning completed his " Dynamics of the Feelings," the book to which he had given the best of these years. It was to be the platform of all his future work. At this particular moment, however, his thoughts were watching no ecstatic molecules in their dance.

The volume he had just laid down was a novel, an old one that he had read before, Jane Eyre. Its power, its energy, its vividness, surprised him. A woman's heart, beating with the passion of love, and held in strong control; that was its burden, its interest, its pathos.

He drew a deep inspiration into his lungs, standing erect. The evening was calm; the scene with so few objects on which the eye could rest, the distant island, the great tract of waters, the setting sun, was impressive on his mind.

Pioneers.

Yes, here on these very seas they sailed,
In battered hulks and groaning timbers,
Beating in the storm;
These ancient mariners; the "sad sincerity" is on
  their brows.
This likes me well—this touch of olden days,
Thoughts that come sweeping on,
The images that rise and fill my mind with heaven and
  earth, and ocean's mighty amplitude,
The feats of high attempt, the peril,
And the new world's won.

·   ·   ·   ·   ·   ·

I.

And who is this upon the barren shore,
Surrounded by his men—Pizarro,
Wrecked, ruined, wretched, mocked of fate.
The look of settled resolution on his face,
The grim, graphic, native humour of his kind,—
His sword's point draws upon the sand a narrow line.
See here my men, this line—
And Northward lies the island we have left—
Beyond is Spain, the dear land of our homes;
Our wives are there, soft smiles and tender names.
There the warm season with its livelong days
Will bring the juicy fruits. . . .
And there secure in ease the days will pass,
The quiet of unnoticed lives—
To die obscure! and be no more.
Now turn from this. What would you share with me?
  Their captain's eye is on them, lo!
Hunger and toil and battle!
No aching limbs must yield, no stout heart fail,
For ever, as we press our onward march,
The savage tracks our way and lurks,—
Eyes of eagles, lions' hearts must then be ours.
Aye, battle! say I, hunger, toil,
Wild savage storms,
But Empire!
Conquest and power, undying fame are ours,—
What ho! Unfurl the standard then,
And raise the cry, Peru!
Empire and the crown of Gold,—
Our battle cry, Peru!

II.

Not these can hold the wild free soldier in his course,
Laws, the force of arms, the tyrant's power,—

The vehement soul is roused, with force meets force,
And rushes to the fray;
With tameless eye, and strong rebellious heart,
I see Balboa charging on the foe—
But now in other mood,
Listening, and with forward straining eye,—
The whispers of another world have come to him—
The story of the seas beyond those mighty cliffs, the
    barriers of the world.
Now soon the tramp of armed men
Disturbs the forest stillness,
And now the patient band —
See where between these rocks it winds its toiling
    upward march,
High in the middle Andes ;
The heights are scaled, the ramparts won !
He pauses and a moment veils his sight.
Beneath him lay —
Nameless, silent, that ocean, eternal.

  .   .   .   .   .   .

Such moments are the kernel of a life,
And bore here, too, their fruit.—
Fell from his soul the dragging chains of vice ;
That recklessness of heart is gone ;
The tumults of the libertine no more ;—
But come the nobler forms of moral worth,
Goodness, and wisdom, justice, self-control.

III.

Lo ! the centuries have fallen,
The temples and the palaces,
The fabrics of the nations' power,
The pomp and panoply of greatness wrecked ;

APPROACHES.

The thoughts that swayed men's lives,
And all the forms of great and small of human acts,
Their struggles and their dreams,
The fevered workings of the under-world,
The pregnant topics of the little day are gone.—

. . . . . .

But here is one of other mien,
A hero as he walks :
This man hath trod the deck at night
And gazed upon the running sea,
And still with worship has uplifted eyes,
Awed, yet sustained by awe :
Free blows the storms !
He bares his breast, exulting in his strength,—Ho
    buffet there !
And nurtures in his heart great visions more than
    dreams :

. . . . .

And now, again, has bent the head in serious thought,
Employed, with patient care, assiduous hand in toil,
Nought lowly that could aid that great attempt;
Rebuffs, the scorn of pride,
The fool's contempt,—these but the good man's lot !—
Yet weary is the pain of fettered limbs,
And heavy is the weight of slow delay,
The gliding years and promise unfulfilled.

. . . . . .

But now the drooping cast is shaken from his mind,
He triumphs even now, disgraced ! a Conqueror !—
For he has heard the low sweet sound of voices in his
    ears,

And seen the visions with his eyes,—
Sweet slumbers too are his,
Toil wins its healthful rest,
And in the glory of the dawn he wakes,—
His senses meet the glad exhilaration of the day,
And in his hero heart has beat the forceful pulse of
    high attempt.

CHAPTER VII.

BRISKETT was walking on the other side, if such a magnificent being could be really said to walk. He rather with a lordly and majestic gait rolled as he moved along; his chest and splendid shoulders, the head carried with unconscious pride and boldness, might have graced a Neptune.

Briskett was a famous swimmer who was travelling to A——. His age was twenty-seven. He had already achieved big feats, but was intending soon, so he said, to eclipse everything ever done before!

The athlete's skin was fine as a woman's; and with his jet black hair, kindly eyes, white even teeth, and regular features, he was very handsome too.

Austin looked at his swaying form with

most unbounded admiration, though something of a smile upon his lips.

Briskett was boasting prodigiously as he rolled with Jarman, a new passenger, arm in arm upon the quarter deck.

Swim, sir ? Austin caught as they passed and repassed, I believe you, sir.—Twenty miles! thirty miles, forty miles, any amount of miles! I could swim all the blessed day and night.—In rough water? In any water. —It's a gift! Some are good at one thing, some at another.—A boy's a boy, a man's a man, and a swimmer's a swimmer!

I don't know except that I have the power and the build.

Chest, yes, 45 inches. Physical cultivation, sir, physical cultivation, that's what you want, and he laughed with boyish good nature.

On the whole perhaps he overrated the power of physical cultivation, for his own magnificent form was rather the healthy growth of one of grand original stock.

There was a free and natural genius in his strength, his face had none of the marks of excessive training. His feet and hands were remarkably well formed, and, like a true Irishman as he was, there was a spontaneous warmth about his grasp. His voice was soft in speech, except when, as now, he boasted like a Colossus; when he sang, and singing in a cathedral had been his previous "sphere," he rolled the deep notes out like thunder. He had "seen life" he had been known mysteriously to say, and knew "what going the pace" meant; still he was simple as a child, and as vain.

Austin saw him strike an attitude that Phidias might have hewn, and with a smile turned to the bulwarks and gazed on the vast expanse of waters and then at the sky above. He could not control his thoughts,—forbidden flights. He could not lead them into intellectual form, he seemed to complain. They rather seemed to buffet him with a warm fervour, to carry him off in their mutiny.

His chest began to heave and his heart to beat with effort.

The sun was setting now, and a heavy

bank of dark clouds had gathered in the west. The slow succeeding growing and dissolving changes with their magnificence and their solemnity impressed him to a calmer mood.

In the deck house sat little Hester Sterne. She was reading there and as Austin turned his head the picture seemed to strike him tenderly. She was absorbed in her book; seriously, diligently, lost to the outer world, the little reader plodded on. One could smile in very sympathy. She was a lively little girl, and had been during the voyage a little spoilt by everyone. Now she looked grave and her features with their intelligence were refined to beauty almost. The wind came gently in and lifted her soft hair about her head, separating it in locks and playing with it in its rise and fall. Hester did not notice it; she turned the leaf, and now and then, still reading, dipped her hand into her pocket and carried pieces of seed cake to her mouth and assiduously munched and read.

Mrs. Sterne, an English lady with pale

thin face, but surely something superior to have so sweet a little girl, was walking up and down for exercise and chatting with the captain. That veteran looked round inquiringly now and then upon the sky. The captain was an Englishman, sturdy, and honest as he looked, dignified, no doubt reserved. The clouds were heavier now, though burnished with the sun's blazing light.

Presently there came the delicate figure of a young girl of about eighteen near the place where Austin was standing and then drew back with a sort of hesitation. Then she walked up again with an air of unconcern, leant over the bulwarks near to where he stood and looked diligently seawards.

Is that the sun over there?

Austin looked at her.

Why yes, said he, and thought the question strange.

Of course it is. But I have been completely puzzled lately. I seem to have lost my way and think the sun ought to be over there, and she pointed diametrically opposite.

O how I wish I was back home again, she cried.

Then why did you come?

Oh, I wished so much to come, and had always looked forward to it. My mother said I ought to go to Dudley for a while and get some polish.

Austin smiled.

But I never had the chance before till just now. Some friends of ours wrote asking me to come to them and saying they would meet me directly the ship arrived, but now although it is only a few days I feel as though I had been separated ever so long from home, and, oh, I have thought how dearly I would like to be back once more to see her only once, to speak to her, to kiss my little brothers and sisters, to play in the garden, to pat the cow and to take a run with Towser—that's our dog.

Why don't you let the tears flow? suggested Austin.

I did! she looked up suddenly surprised and blushing.

And felt relieved?

Yes, I felt relieved but then again—here she became graver—sometimes it comes upon me suddenly and makes me fearful,—I feel as though I will never see them again.

Oh, no, cheer up. No doubt everyone feels that for a while on leaving home, especially for the first time, but now you must look a little into the future. Think what a fine girl you will be when you return!

Ah, I don't like to look even at the future now. When I first came on board I felt miserable and lonely to be all amongst strangers. The first morning I saw you you looked so serious, I thought I would be always afraid to speak to you.

Now I've got to know the people here, or at least got used to their faces and their ways, and to meeting them and chatting together on the deck and in the cabin, it seems to be like another separation then to have to leave and—and she blushed again as she added confidentially, I could let the tears flow again.

Well there's no great harm in that, but if you weep, weep in secret.

Yes, yes, so I did, that is, of course—I must go down. It is beginning to get cold and I think a storm is coming on.

Austin returned to his cabin to read, but it was drawing near the end now, and people became extraordinarily confidential on board ship.

Jarman had asked him to talk about Spencer.

That's all very well, said he interrupting Austin's exordium, but I would like to know how you are going to get that to the masses.

I probably couldn't get that to the masses, said Austin laughing. He had not got it to Jarman.

But if it's a religion? explained J.

But perhaps it is not a religion! Suppose that a man losing faith in the traditions of the elders set himself down at last to think his own way out and, after years of toil and faithful service and with what help he could gather, found a track and a dim glimmering of light, but still a guide, a recompense; and if in the deep feelings of this solacement he had told another and comforted him too, and others had also learnt this and been comforted, is not that in itself good? And if Spencer were but such a one and his thoughts had gone abroad and been received by those who were truthful and understood and were thankful, were it altogether apt to say—this a religion! and how are you to get it to the masses?

How do we get our Christian religion to the masses? Do they finely speculate and whet their wits on that most imminent of paradoxes, Three in One, or read their Bible exegetically. The newer Philology—do they call that into service and the fine points of Christian Evidences? I am amazed. In what one respect, in the individual life, or the colossal machine of the nation, is our civilization built on the words of Christ. The sermon on the mount: the web of society—the comparison of one with the other is not within the region of sanity. What has been done in the progress of the world has been done by the great minds in science, literature, public life, amid nations moulded originally on the one great Right of Force, and whose imperfect institutions of freedom have arisen from the wild efforts to fling off outworn tyrannies.

The masses, all men, are governed on every hand by forces that they wot not of—Philosophy, opinion, the adjustment of ten thousand interests, the "rules of the game" of force and selfishness, move the machine at top, from thence in lower grades, laws, constitutions, institutions, forms of intercourse, in thousand shapes, until the grooves are made in which your masses feel the press.

The oracle is understood, interpreted.

The Word goes forth, descending, spreading. Poets sing it, Authors write it, Painters paint it, Newspapers print it, your Masses make it their vernacular.

Jarman was listening in great impatience.

Ah yes, but what we want is the great principle of brotherhood. I'm a philosopher. A Spencerian too in fact. I go further though. There are many things I'm more advanced than you in. I'm a thorough-going Socialist. I'm a declared Atheist, although I was brought up in the strictest set of the Pharisees, and my father's a bishop. I'm a Pessimist too, God knows it's no wonder, everything, all sorts of things like that! Are you?

No, said Austin demurely. You are more advanced than I am. I almost think that that garment of your soul is too fantastic. There is safety in a swallow tail!

Down with conventionalities up with philosophy! cried Jarman. I have differentiated myself up to a great extent! I hate all sham, all conventionalities—Government, Property, Religion, Marriage—everything. I'd rather have an intellectual mistress than a wife; and if I were married, and my wife loved another and he had got the key to her room, I could look on with philosophic calm! I have brought myself so far. I have differentiated myself up to that.

A mysterious, perhaps a philosophic, smile, passed over the features of the differentiated man.

Yes, he continued, down with all conventionalities and up with philosophy. The world is sunk beyond our power!

Now take a woman like Mrs. Sterne, a woman well brought up, as people say, educated, plays the piano well. She can talk chit chat all day long, and the wretched small change of conventionality. She told me that she regarded Barclay the second mate as a fine stamp of man—a complete ass—without two consecutive ideas, with no ideas at all as one might say, popularly speaking—I suppose fellows of that stamp have a sort of courage of their own—and I'm inclined to overrate that, for I'm constitutionally timid myself, but I can never place the animal above the intellectual!

I say, Jarman, old boy, was heard a voice outside the door, are you there? We want you for a four-handed Euchre.

Right, Barclay, I'll be there directly. Well, Brandt, old man, we'll be in the Bay by this time to-morrow night, eh? We've had some interesting discussions together and mustn't lose sight of each other when we step ashore. I've gained some respect for your learning, I'll own that—but I could never value your judgment.

How so ? Austin inquired.

Because you don't believe in Spiritualism. You are not differentiated up to that. You never show up in so bad a light as —

Jarman, damn your eyes, are you going to take a hand or not ?

Right, Barclay, old fellow, I'm there.

By this time to-morrow they would be in the Bay, and within another twenty-four hours he would be home again. Home. The news of his mother's death—it was that had hastened his return.

Susan was married, and from her too he had received, long ago, a letter saying that Faith Shenstone was engaged.

He had read. It was as though some form of power had vanished out of him. He had gone to his window and in his lonely room had stood there motionless. And familiar things were like unreal pageants. He wandered in the Prado at night, and sat down at last on a bench hiding his face in his hands. How lonely seems to have been my life. . . . And in that night he had sought to elevate his mind. O let never wandering thoughts of mine imagine less happiness to her. And next morning he had resumed or tried to resume his work.

It was gradually that a sense of loss, of desolation, came into his mind. He had smiled, my dreams and fairy tales for ever gone, and looked at some scattered papers he had taken from his desk.

They were fragments addressed, Faith.

In silence their inspiration had come, in silence he had felt their power, in silence now must their whole record close.

Was there a day he had not thought of her? No, not an hour, she did not hover near at least.

Words, phrases, songs, familiar—we know their meaning, feel their sense—and, lo, an experience arises, an occasion, a change, a new meaning leaps out of the words, a strange depth is unveiled, we see into the poet's heart.

> Maiden with the soft brown eyes
> In whose orb a shadow lies
> Standing with unwilling feet
> Where the brook and river meet.

I'm sitting by the stile, Mary
Where we sat side by side —

Stranger, if thou hast ever felt the loneliness,
The silence, unregarded tears,
Amid the universe, a child, wayfarer —

And when he sat in quiet, still in his unescapable solitudes, shutting out recollections, and bending his mind to its tasks, suddenly wild thoughts would fountain up and rush in hot streams through his brain as of the struggles of a life of feeling that he had attempted to stifle in the mechanical works of the intellect. Now. He turned over the leaves and read them here and there. The warmth that gave life was wanting now; they seemed unreal.

If I were to write to you, Faith, every time I have traced your image and filled my heart with sweet love to the brim.

We will never part again, then, Faith?

Sadness—You standing by me—Life streams into me with that touch. You are my life, my sweetest life.

Even to have written this has lightened my heart again.

We must both love something better than ourselves.

Our own love will be raised for we will have raised ourselves.

Courage is not born of hate but love.

This is our pilgrimage—to develop our life to bring back the prizes of a rightful prowess, to have accomplished ourselves to do the work that aids, ennobles others too, and wins from them glad sympathy —

The heart can famish, and oppressive thoughts that beat upon the brain steal into the pilgrim's tent —

Sweet minister of Grace. Sweet Faith. Sweet wife.

He had sealed them and put them away.

A knock was heard at the door. Austin closed his book and threw his shoulders back as the genial Briskett entered.

That athletic hero was a sociable being, and was apt to become somewhat heavy in mind when left alone.

Busy?

Nay, sit thee down, I have been thinking to-night a little about old times, not studying.

Always reading and thinking and puzzling things out, said Briskett, half admiringly and half disapprovingly shaking his head.

I don't read so much as you suppose, said Austin amused. But do I look like dying, that you shake your head at me so ominously?

No, that's what puzzles me —

It's a gift, said Austin laughing. Briskett, you are not badly made. I think I'll take your measurements, 45 round the chest, eh ? And round the calf?

Round the calf he returned seriously, half apologetically not so good only 16½, but 17 round the biceps. Look here and he doubled up his arm.

Pooh, I want to see you in the buff. I'll test these measurements myself. I have seen some splendidly made fellows here and there, though, no doubt, of slighter build than you.

Briskett's chest arched out magnificently, grandly ribbed, compact and solid, and clad with masses of swelling muscle! Austin noted in complete detail, observing the play of the various muscles in movement, and felt his skin, noticed its lively colour, and the firmness of its texture, pinched him, struck him blows, listened to his heart beats, made him draw in deep breaths, and exhale quickly and slowly again and again, all the while simmering in delight.

Briskett's arms seemed almost to lose natural shape from their enormous size. Flattered by Austin's admiration he braced himself up and stood in fighting attitude, tossing his head back and then swinging his arms about in huge reaches and efforts, while his eyes began to shine with a sort of warlike fire.

Splendid! and Austin took him by the hands and looked at him.

Briskett seized him by the waist and held him up aloft as one might dance a child.

Austin bared his own arm. White and very slender it looked beside the swimmer's Samson limb.

Briskett grasped it with a grip like a vice.

Oh well, he said at length, I've seen worse. That arm is not so badly shaped. Hard enough too, and in the pink of condition. But—but— You must leave these books of yours altogether, and go in for physical cultivation.

I'm afraid I've used my muscles too much like slaves and they have given me but slavish service.

Very well then, go to bed now, don't rack your brains any more to-night, and I'll call you early in the morning to see land.

So saying he laid his hand solemnly on Austin's shoulder, looked at him with great admiration, shook hands and departed. He returned immediately he had closed the door, popped his head in, uttered the words " physical cultivation ! " and departed laughing abundantly.

CHAPTER VIII.

MEANWHILE the storm had been steadily rising; a continued sound of rolling and bumping and crashing was going on above.

Austin, however, was soon asleep, and was next suddenly aroused by a peculiar shake and lurching of the ship. Sounds of unusual scurrying, and as though of some confusion, soon were heard.

Briskett in shirt and trousers came rushing in.

Jump up, old fellow, quick! B' Jupiter, it's the screw we've broke. I want to see where we are.

Austin leapt up. A panic struck through him, paralyzing all his faculties,—death!— the thought swept in, a storm struggled and rose in his mind, then excitement, and a fearful tension. Up the steps in terror he ran—the fierce cold wind as he emerged on deck dashed the spray in gusts and splashes on his face. Through the dim grey he looked out into the sea—mad waves, mad waves! Staggering along holding on by what he could, struck by the drenching masses of water that every now and then burst on the ship and made it shake again, he reached at length a drier and securer place.

Meanwhile his panic had been lost,—holding on was desperate work enough and that absorbed for a while his attention.

The billows came sweeping down upon the ship as though to overwhelm so frail a fabric in their mass. The vessel rose, the waters seemed to burst from under her and, as she bounded, staggered, trembled, bore themselves along, majestic, swift in march like a conquering host, then, succeeded by the next, were swallowed in the night.

Austin looked steadily, and with a desperate effort gained his self control. His utter helplessness, the grandeur of the scene striking through the caverns of his mind, raised all that was supreme within. He gazed calmly now, and as the prospect soon grew more distinct, saw, with a transient disappointed recognition that the storm was not so great as he had thought; the waves were long in sweep, and not broken, but regular. The ship was lurching, and tossing, and pitching and sometimes as he expected her to right, would suddenly plunge again as if to be engulfed,—the waters striking her with tremendous force, a flood rushing on the deck.

Like a massy wall or series of mountain ridges it seemed of waters, that, from the ship-side springing, with their wild assertive triumph swept away—while unconsciously he kept crying out, ho! ho! then another, ho!—then another, then another, then another, succeeding and vanishing in the dark — thought swirled at sense of these tremendous powers at play, the boundless vast of waters moved,—the billowing flood scarps leaping to the clouds, the endless sea in storm. Storm, storm, storm, from horizon to horizon, the huge bubbling boiling billows, from horizon to horizon, storm, storm, storm.

* * * *

Brandt, good God, where are you? cried Briskett, breaking on the scene, I've been looking for you everywhere. Your life belt, have you one?

No.

Downstairs and get one then, and wrap your blankets round you too if we are going to stay here. It's no use knocking under till we've kicked the last kick, and many's the worse sea I've seen than this.

Briskett himself descended again saying that he wanted to get a rope. Austin with great difficulty made his way along. The blankets would be a comfort. To talk of life-belts sounded rather like a grim joke.

On the stairs he met the captain coming down, clad in oil-skin with the big hat that nearly shrouded his face. His jaws seemed locked in iron resolution, his eyes were set.

Austin looked at him as they met, a light came to the captain's eyes, revealing all the unspeakable world of such moments. He brusquely passed on, and Austin mounted.

A fearful scene was going on meanwhile.

The passengers most of them had rushed in scanty raiment on the deck, others were driven by the rude buffeting waters back, each encountering at every turn the panic on his neighbour's face.

The captain and the officers did all they could to restore, not confidence, but yet some form of order in the startled herd.

The faint streakings of early day were now beginning to appear; and soon the light was clearer. And with the pale light, and the grey tinges mixed with the shadowings of dusk, and the ominous gloom of a cloudy ridge, a picture was limned out,— titanic. The dawn broke quickly, the shadows seemed to scatter and melt.

There on the lee was showing, and fearfully close it seemed with the vessel drifting on, yes, spite of all that sails could do, there was no mistaking that, a terrible spectacle— a vast and rockbound shore.

She won't be long striking. Look here,

said Briskett, stay by me, we'll keep the stern of the ship. There they are all rushing to the front, they think they will be nearer to the land!

The sky was now lifted somewhat—the light became still clearer. Some of the passengers were veritably mad, and in panic everyone. Some fell down and prayed aloud. Some cursed, and shook their fists at the captain in their rage. Some mingled prayers and curses, and rushed about, and shrieked, and rent their garments.

Austin looked in vain for Hester and her mother, they must have stayed below; Miss Halley had appeared on deck—half-dressed, wrapped in blankets, her hair falling in long dishevelled streamers from her head. She looked steadily upon the scene, seemed to have no terror, seemed to be absorbed in contemplation—prayer he afterwards thought it might have been. Presently she began to sing. Low at first it was and as though to herself, the words were undistinguishable.

Then her voice broke out loud and clear, "There's a land that is brighter than day."

She seemed as if inspired, and threw her whole soul into the old familiar hymn. Above the tempest's buffetings her voice rose high. Again and again as she stood there, wrapped in the white sheet, with streaming hair, like one possessed, panting it out, the volume of pure sound rose upon the wind.

She had ceased—a peril imminent at once and fearful held all now in suspense. The ship seemed to rush to meet her fate. A huge billow bore her. With a superb spring, a sort of triumphant carriage, she bounded on the rock, a tremendous crash, and every fibre shook. She lurched round, toppled over, and then seemed to become fixed in the crags.

The passengers had all made way to the front. Some of the sailors attempted to lower boats; they were dashed to fragments.

Austin Brandt, cried Briskett, we have one chance left.

What is that?

It is possible to swim this.

Austin shook his head.

For you. Wait. The ship may hold together. For me!

Look here on this side. This sea is not hopeless at all. There in the front—madness! The water is dashed into foam. Here though from where we stand the waves are high, but they are unbroken and have a long swell. We can do it here.

I. No. I could not live a minute there.

I will save you, said Briskett steadily.

No, no, cried Austin. Useless! I will wait. The ship may hold.

No chance. She is straining and bumping like mad and look there—she's breaking up amid-ships.

So she was. The water battering at her there had begun to make a clean breach through.

The passengers were clinging to the rigging and bulwarks for support; they stood drenched, half drowned by the spray.

Barclay had carried Hester in his arms and had lashed her to the rigging and wrapped his own great coat around her.

The captain no longer gave orders, but

stood there with a settled look upon his face, and watched the waters do their worst.

Come, said Briskett abruptly, there's no time to lose. Here let me hitch that life belt up! It would be whipped off in a brace of shakes.

He made the life belt secure.

Where is your own?

I will not use one, the swimmer replied, I think it's best not for me. Now come let me tie this rope round you and then I'll lash you on my back.

No, Briskett, no, cried Austin, it cannot be. Alone you might save yourself, but burdened with my weight upon your back. No.

With you I can do it! but to leave you here! No. A coward's heart would never bear me to that shore.

Without more ado, he tied the rope round Austin's waist then round his shoulders and finally lashed him tightly to himself.

Destruction was rife, meanwhile. The ship seemed in two; both parts were shaking terribly. Austin watched everything. The sea, the ship, the passengers, every circumstance had etched itself upon his brain. Miss Halley seemed again to be singing, though he could not catch the sound. She alone preserved her firmness, but it seemed as though she could not trust herself to view the horror of the scene—she poured forth all her voice singing with desperate force.

Austin's heart smote him.

See Briskett, said he, save her. A woman, a delicate girl. Leave me. It is unmanly for me to need your help. Save her. Save her. It can be done. The waters have gone down. See how evenly these waves swell, sweeping down to yonder point.

The point was about a quarter of a mile away where the coast took a short sweep outwards forming a little bay and ending in a point. All the coast straight ahead and up to the point was battered by the wildest surge.

Briskett's eyes had been busy on this side. He had long ago observed the point and formed his resolutions. He looked now towards the ship again. No, he cried. It can't be done. I could never reach the bows. Madness! See how the flood is rushing in between. It would fling me on to the rocks like a log of wood. And even then —

No. I'll save you, no other.

Several of the sailors had attempted to make their way by swimming to the shore. They were the veriest toys. Some seemed to sink at once, others appeared again still swimming—but not long.

A few moments afterwards Miss Halley herself was seen to leave the side. A cry went up.

The third officer had leapt in after her. He was a splendidly built fellow, a lion. Both wore life belts. They were borne along the crest of a huge billow for a while. A floating mass carrying wreckage was seen to strike the rescuer. They were gone.

The bows had now careened over from the weather side.

Mrs. Sterne clinging with might and main to the rigging called loudly to her child. She was dead. The ship gave a lurch, she herself was flung into the boiling waves. Barclay sprang in after her; he had no hope to save her. Both were lost in an instant. The end was close at hand. Briskett had been still watching the billows that swept from the stern.

Look, he cried. Every now and then we get one right up here that seems to sweep away to yonder point. She'll smash up directly.

Watch for the next—when I give the signal take the water with me. Keep your mouth shut. Don't lose heart. It can be done. Ah, look, Austin, go!

In a moment Austin felt swept along with fearful force. He clung to consciousness. To struggle was mere helplessness.

The swimmer was making prodigious efforts under him. That hero's heart had never quailed. He had foreseen all this, and was putting forth all his strength.

Austin too bent every faculty.

Desperate was the struggle, but the billows were smoother nearing the point. It was a matter of hard work simply.

In rounding it would be the crux.

Once that cleared they were safe. The set of the waves was there and they carried the burden on. The water became broken again, but he must not get out too far. He toiled and did not flag. A few seconds would decide the bout. The critical moment came. He was flinging all his strength into the work and fought like Hercules.

The point was rounded, the water was much calmer there. His strokes were almost powerless now.

Spent and done, with the strength dying in his heart, he could do little more than keep himself afloat. The waves rolled in upon the sandy beach, a long billow carried the humans up its slope. Briskett with his last remaining strength dug hands and feet deep in the sand to hold against the back wash. He remained fast, then crawling, reached a higher spot before the next came. They were safe.

But he lay there motionless, exhausted, dying.

Austin recovered first. The waves had

beaten him almost senseless and as they reached the land he swooned away.

Painfully, with struggling recollections he revived, stared round, then comprehended all. Exhausted, sick, he could have closed his eyes and slept, but that would be the sleep of death.

He must act. The cords had swelled with the water and bound him painfully tight. To undo them was impossible. He had not strength to try. Presently looking round, he espied a sharp piece of flint within reach, and with this laboriously cut through the strands.

Briskett's face was ghastly, his whole frame inanimate.

Briskett, Briskett, old fellow, called Austin kneeling beside him, are you too weak to rise? See here, this coast is inhabited. I will try and reach a house and get assistance. I can do nothing for you now. You must wait till I come back. He seized Briskett's hand. Have you understood?

Briskett faintly opened his eyes, faintly

grasped Austin's hand, and sank back again. Austin brushed the wet hair from his forehead and kissed him.

Dragging himself painfully along a few steps, he paused from sheer exhaustion. A brief struggle passed over him lest the very spirit should be yielded. Hope was sinking. His life seemed ebbing out. A fit of sickness was followed by a choking thirst. He lay motionless, then painfully dragging his body he reached a tiny rill of water formed from the recent rain. A blessing to the weary one it was; faint, almost nerveless, he struggled on.

Gradually his strength and spirit both revived. A stout stick picked up helped him much, and stumbling on a track the hope of succour made the walking easier. He warmed up and trudged stoutly enough.

Cast upon my native shore, naked, dying, the labour of years behind, possessions swallowed in the waves; marry, that was a shrewd stroke.

What have I here? My naked self and all that in me is.

Touched bottom. Ha! Then every step leads upward now!

My native land. Now I could throw myself upon its bosom and like a foolish being kiss the earth. An image of a young giant comes before me, lusty, resolute, free. Truly there is a glory in these blue skies; and what is this form of a woman, beautiful, free, with a spirit beating as though with the beating of wings. I behold. It is the Winged Victory.

* * * * *

The road led through a gate. Within the fence were sheep and cattle. Soon a homestead showed its cheer. The milkmaid had been, though so early, bathing her face in the morning dew. Fresh increase of milk, her prize and her pride, she bore in the pail on her head. She was setting out buxomly homeward, singing away in her innocent freedom.

What, Ho! Hallo!

She turned with a scream, the milkpail fell, the maid began to scurry off.

Shipwrecked! he yelled with might and main.

She heard and stopped threw off her ample apron, and ran then to the house.

The apron Austin received like a blessing, and presently as he approached two men came towards him, one of them bringing blankets. One of the men a great brown bushy bearded fellow whom his companion called Bob wrapped the blankets round him, they carried him to the house and put him there to bed.

Bob rubbed his chest and arms talking cheerfully the while, and something was being prepared for him to eat.

A middle aged and buxom little woman brought in a steaming bowl with a sort of motherly fussiness. Boiled sago it was, with warm diluted wine poured over it. Austin found he could eat a little—it was very good —and soon began to feel his spirits rise again.

He had told them of Briskett at the first and had described the way. The men had caught and harnessed a couple of horses. Austin insisted on going with them, though the good woman opined he looked more like going to Heaven. They took with them now a spring cart, too, so that as far as the way was accessible they might bring it, and this would be better for Briskett returning.

They approached the shore where both had been cast up; Austin dreaded to find his faithful companion dead.

They turned the corner of a rock. He was gone. There was no one to be seen. Marks were there, however, they saw as they arrived at the spot, as though he had crawled away on hands and knees, and soon they traced them towards a little sand hummock, and under this in what little shelter could be found, lay Briskett's torso there.

His arms and legs were deadly white; an incessant shivering gave the only, doleful, sign of life. They placed him in the blankets and rubbed his limbs, and gave him brandy to drink. For a full hour they applied themselves to him before it was safe to take him from the spot. The trembling in all his limbs continued long after they had brought him home.

The strange expedition was gone.

At the gate the women were waiting. At their head stood one, by manner and dress a lady. The curious tale was being told her, exaggerated, wonderful. She could listen no longer and wait, curious, eager, pitying, moved with strange interest, they followed the wheel track, she leading. They walked fast; approaching the sea shore the marks were deep in the sand. A wild light had come into her eyes. She moved faster, a wild thought was urging her step, she ran. The hat was blown off, the hair fluttered down, and streamed out behind in the wind. She had reached the top of the mound. Her gaze swept the coast. She raised herself. She tottered. A wild cry rung on her lips. She covered her face with her hands, staggered backwards, and fell.

There in the hollow below was the group. Bob was rubbing the chest of the swimmer. Sandy was giving him brandy. Close by, of the colour of death, wrapped in his blanket, reclining, was Austin.

Martha raised her mistress, calling her Mary. She had seen at a glance.

H'sh. Recover yourself! Return to the house lest he see you. Yes. I will do all.

Mrs. Greenway, the fussy little woman of the sago and wine, took Briskett in charge. In Mrs. Neville's own house a room was prepared for Austin. The doctor who lived in the village eight miles away, was sent for, post haste.

CHAPTER IX.

It was the afternoon, and Austin had fallen asleep.

Mary slipped to his room unobserved. Of course she had heard the wondrous tale. Open-eyed she had listened. Here was indeed a romance. She was fluttering all the day.

With finger on lip she opened the door and, tip-toe, looked in. The chamber was still, her movements were mouselike. She stood long gazing, holding her breath, absorbed, then crept softly back, closed the door, and ran off to tell her Mama.

Mama, Mama, I saw him. His face was white!

Mary! Never again go near that room! No. No, my child—but you know that sick people must not be disturbed, and you will not, if I ask you.

Austin was not so bad, the doctor said. Good nursing would bring him round.

The swimmer lay helpless, the life within him unsteadily flickering. The doctor had only mournful news. A magnificent fellow he said, I never saw the like—never—but—

He listened to the story of the rescue again. Mrs. Greenway described Austin's ghost-like appearance when first she had seen him—but all the time, she said, he seemed to be breaking his heart for the other.

The other, said the doctor, has broken his heart for him.

It was many days after this that Austin was sitting by Briskett's bedside. The swimmer was sad and held Austin's hand and often pressed it warmly. He deemed it but his duty done to have saved another's life. There is a naïveté in all true heroism.

Stop, he said, interrupting, I'm filled with a great joy for what I've done! then he added, perhaps I have saved myself. Who knows? I got into fast company with this swimming business. I'm rid of it now. Rid of it. Rid of it for ever. I thank God for it. Many a time on the old ship when we used to talk together what you said went deeper than you thought. That life had a sort of intoxication, I suppose it was that. I'm rid of it now.

A strange idea has come into my head. My brother you know, I told you, is a clergyman in New York. Has one of the largest churches there. Splendid voice he has. Fills the whole church. I think I'll go back to him and study up for it too. I was meant for that, but while he was always at his books, I was out riding or fishing—fly fishing—did you ever fly fish?

No.

The best sport in the whole world. You must have the right fly you know and have a bit of knack —

Well you'll go back to your brother.

No. We didn't get on so well as we ought. I see now it was my fault. I'll go to my uncle. I know I'm a favourite of his in spite of all. Yes I'll go to him. I've been getting into dangerous company—that's the truth. This has settled me. I suppose I'll never be good for anything now, eh? in the athletic line? I trained with Billy Mitchell in New York. I showed you Billy's portrait, you know. Billy and I saw life. Whoop, those were the times, and he raised himself up suddenly. I used to think—

He ceased in a moment. He had fainted away.

Austin called and Mrs. Greenway and Sarah with much fuss and circumstance brought him to at last.

Briskett could not realize at first how weak he was. These fainting fits of his, however, warned him at length. He would refer then to his change of mental habit. He would go to his uncle and under his guidance devoutly study for the Church. He was firm in this resolution.

Poor old fellow, he used to lie there so quietly and smile so good naturedly when anyone entered the room, and for every little favour show himself so pleased, and seemed to wish only not to be left alone. It was touching.

Briskett had written to his uncle and had received a most encouraging reply. He was anxious to go, though to leave the farmhouse was a wrench. He said that though his strength was gone, this brief time seemed the happiest of all. He looked well enough and with his colossal frame extorted Mary's utmost admiration. She thought him better than the hero of her last story, who though extraordinarily endowed in feature and physique had a more than Corsair fierceness.

Briskett though he had been a foolish young man would not wittingly have hurt a spider. He was much inclined to friendly offices, and really, Mary seriously thought, this is nicer in the round of daily life. Mary used to like to hear him talk of his late exploits and Briskett boasted terribly, while Mary listened, and expanded her imagination open eyed. Then he used to get excited a little, and afterwards his heart would weakly flutter, and when she knew of this she would not listen to those stirring tales again.

So different you both are, Mary confided to Austin one day, he is so brave and great, and has seen so much, and you are so more like every day.

Poor Briskett had to say good-bye at last; he came back three several times to shake hands again, and there was great waving of handkerchiefs till he was out of sight.

Mary averred that she saw tears standing in his eyes.

The seriously inclined champion had given Austin a volume of Paley's Evidences which his uncle had sent him to read.

He had not read more than a page or two but in the fly leaf had inscribed a little legend of one who had a violin which he loved, the story ran, too dearly, and finally to purify his heart had broken. There seemed no thoroughly reasonable cogent argument expressed why he should so have slain the tuneful voice, but Austin guessed that the swimmer here played on a struggle nearer home.

Mary declared he gave her an idea of what an ancient knight was like. She began to plot a story full of chargers, nodding plumes, and courtly chivalry. The heroine was to be an Arabian Princess, who had spent much time in sighing for her ideal and found it, alas!—a Paladin.

CHAPTER X.

TENDER hands had smoothed Austin's pillow, faithful eyes had outwatched the night, as he had lain there, feverish, weak, with the life burning low.

It was with a happy feeling of health he awoke one day, and looked around. Fever and pain had vanished; his spirit was light. And he sat up in bed, and looked half amused, at his nurse. She was sitting with a book on her knee, but the patient eyes were veiled, the weary lids had closed.

The motherly face wore good records, constancy, courage; his smile was more grave. Then curiously puzzling, he seemed to have known the face.

He looked, turned his head, looked.

Martha!

She awoke springing up, and making a sign to be still, smoothed the pillow again.

No, no, Martha. What is this? I demand to know. Who sent you here? Tell me. Tell me. Did *she* send you here. Nay, but I will rise even now, and depart at once from this house.

Martha was fluttering, weeping. The door opened, and covering her face with her hands, Mrs. Neville came hurriedly in and dropped on her knees by the bedside, taking his hand in hers, bowed herself down, and pressed the hand to her forehead.

I beg, do not speak! It will harm you. Be patient, still; and when you are stronger then we will talk of it all.

No, no, said Austin, sinking back on the pillow from weakness. Speak now. You must. My sickness is gone. I am calm. Rise.

She was weeping. He added gently, Nay, then, but rise and tell me all about this. I would have called on you at Ferndale House.

Ferndale House! What! . . . You knew
—you knew of his death?
Yes, I read that. Did you then leave
Ferndale House?
Mrs. Neville told him briefly of the state
of her affairs at her husband's death. She
did not tell him of Mary, nor of her own
bitter struggle at first with sickness, poverty,
care. In a few years, it appeared, the land
on which her little cottages had stood had
increased in value—such increments were
common enough at that time—fifty-fold.

She had repurchased the farm, that had
belonged to her once long ago, and had built
for herself, near the homestead, this cottage
in which they were living.

* * * * *

Now she resumed her duties as nurse.
Gentle she was, and patient and good.
Whether she talked, or read, one could have
listened for hours to that sweet voice.

It was a grateful sense to feel her presence
near.

"Gentle nurse" he used to call her; and
now and then with something of her old

archness, she would dress like a servant-maid, bringing in his tea and toast, and drop a curtsey, and the quaint smile would ripple beneath the sad cast of the face.

And as day by day slipped by, and he felt happy only when she was near, and admired her the more, he fell into weaker musings.

Here am I still, secluded, unknown, unhonoured. After so many years. My book was to make me famous—where is the record of those years of loneliness—my " Dynamics of the Feelings," the wild sea has swallowed. And now here—Fame is but a weak solicitation. Sweet would be a life of meditation—where?

The feelings of tenderness with which he regarded his " Gentle Nurse " were not unmixed with others, that swept him away from her wildly.

Did Mrs. Charlwood never say a word to you of me? she asked one day. Dr. Charlwood assisted me with my affairs. Yes it was due to him to say that; they were all unselfish in their kindness, but—I felt strange, altered, wished to escape.

I never saw her afterwards. I was disturbed in mind, avoided her. How is she? She was a good woman spoiled, but I hope at least she is, as the world goes, happy.

She is dead!

Dead!

Yes. Oh, Austin it was awful. She was a good woman—spoiled, I can scarcely speak of it. You knew her weakness, did you not? Oh it was his conduct drove her to it first. That brought all ruin in its train. She drank the more to stifle recollections. And then the shame of it all would come upon her. I have seen her as I hope never to see another—hating herself, the vilest wretch on earth, she would say. And then again she would drink herself into good spirits, and laugh at her "maudlin tears."

"Now up, now down," she would say, "that's the salad to the dish." . . . The end, how can I tell it. . . . She seemed to have lost reason —

* * * * *

It was in the days of convalescence that

his gentle nurse was dearer to him than ever.

Why, Austin, she said, laughing, after tea, it is only a few days since you were lying there so white and meek, and now your eyes are beginning to burn.

He had taken her hand, and kissed her cheek; she was grave in a moment, had drawn her head away, stood with eyes cast down. Then she left him, and drew to the window. Austin looked, and his heart smote him.

Remembrances of the past came like a cloud.

I have wronged you, he said. She came gently to his side and pressed his hand.

Wickedly, bitterly. I know how noble your true nature was. I have made you unhappy.

Her voice was gentle.

No, Austin. Let us not speak so now. I am not unhappy now. . . . These last few days—have been so sweet—that they have seemed—to atone for all.

He broke hastily away. From eyes, that for long years had forgotten to weep, the hot tears streamed.

I hate myself! Remorse for that has come on me —

Austin, do not! do not! do not live on that bitter past. It is morbid. That past is gone. Fix your thoughts on what is before. You have work to do. It would be wrong, it would be folly to sacrifice any part of that, to let the Evil rob further from the Good.

* * * * *

And the next day she entered smiling.

She had brought the prettiest posy of flowers from her garden—" To Austin, on his Birthday," and her eyes glistened.

I had not remembered it, he said, leaping up, and looking almost thunderstruck. The years that are gone, and nothing done. All at once I feel the need of fresh air. The years that are gone, and nothing done!—

He went out and saddled a horse and with some difficulty mounted.

Always headstrong, she said, quaintly reproving, looking up at his face, with her hand on the rein of his horse.

The cool air, the fatigue, brought relief. He rode by the sea shore, the wreckage still strewed the beach.

Three of the sailors had actually swam that fearful night to land. Two had been smashed on the rocks. The third had escaped from the waves, had proceeded some paces and then perhaps had stumbled and been stunned by the fall. He had been found drowned, face downward, in a little shallow pool in the rock.

Austin recalled the voyagers' faces. Miss Halley, innocent, brave; the philosopher, Jarman; Barclay, the mate; and little Hester Sterne—all drowned.

Verily the reward of virtue is virtue; of swimming, swimming. I must be up and doing, he cried.

Mrs. Neville was in her garden when Austin rode slowly up again.

She was stooping occasionally as though tending a shrub, and looked up constantly towards the window beyond the verandah. A little girl was sitting there, and Mrs. Neville observing her look turned round. The blood had rushed to her face, she knew not whither to avert it.

Well, said Austin laughing as she came out. You look disappointed at seeing me safely returned.

But do not wait. It is cold, Austin, I beseech you. You are not strong enough yet, and I —

Austin was laughing. Are you entertaining an angel unawares? Or who is that little girl behind the window. Never did I see a face so beautiful. She'll be jumping through the pane too directly to come out. This is the land of happy children. He beckoned.

The little girl disappeared and then came running out with a cap upon her head, and a sort of plaid about her. She clung as though half hiding to Mrs. Neville's dress, but none the less looked up to Austin steadily.

Well little girl, said he, won't you shake hands with me?

He lifted up the light hair and played with its fineness, and patted her cheek and smiled as he looked in her eyes.

And who tied this shawl so daintily about you?

Martha.

Martha, that was very good of Martha to wrap you up like—like—no, not exactly like Little Red Riding Hood—but, what's your name first?

Mary.

Mary, ah, a good name. Mary, Mary quite contrairy, how does your garden grow? With cockle shells and silver bells and—how then does it go? Do you know all about that little Mary?

Oh yes, long ago. I know ever so many Marys.

Well?

Well, there was Mary the Mother of Jesus and Mary —

Mary! It's cold! Inside quick, without a word! See if Martha is getting tea ready.

Poor little Mary had made a great effort

to break off, just as she was getting into swing with the other Marys.

Austin suddenly drew her to him and kissed her.

A sweet little girl, a beautiful face—full of intelligence and life. Didn't she scud away when I kissed her! Good little girl. I hope her kisses will always be as fairly given as that. . . .

Mary. But Mary what? he asked, reining his horse.

Mrs. Neville raised her face. She approached.

Good God! What? Speak! say it, say it.

She took his hands tightly, and she leant her head on the saddle, then looked up.

I cannot say it! He turned his rein, and galloped over the hills again till physical exhaustion had stifled the pain of the mind.

CHAPTER XI.

MARTHA was tying the child's hair with a ribbon when he entered the room.

He took Mary's two hands in his, and gazed earnestly into her face. Mary seriously, earnestly, gazed at him. Martha slipped out of the room. Mrs. Neville looked at the two.

Little Mary, sweet little girl. Tell me now were you angry that I kissed you yesterday?

Mary looked up shyly, first to him and then to her mother.

No, she said, I was not angry.

That's good.

And we will go for a nice walk to-day; your Mama and Martha and you, and I? See how beautiful it is outside. I wish to talk to your Mama about old times, and we'll take a walk by the sea beach, eh? And you and Martha can pick up the pretty shells. We'll see "the dainty tint that oft appears on rosy shells." Do you get many nice ones here?

Oh, yes, sometimes, that is, not so nice as I thought they would be. But I like to see the waves coming in. It is great fun. And once we saw a great ship away far out, didn't we, Mama? We watched it till it was out of sight. I was wondering where it was going and who were the people. And I thought of the Mayflower when John Alden was about to embark and caught sight of Priscilla.

Something she seemed to be pondering.

It is indeed sad to say the parting word— you know, Mama —

The mother seemed to know —

And will you not give me a kiss too, before we go out?

Austin held the little hand while they walked to the beach. Trustfully it rested in his and the little girl danced and trotted full of spirits. Mary and Martha were gathering their shells. The mother told the tale of Mary, all sorts of little incidents, too, treasured up. She did not tell of sleepless nights, the weary days, the tears in secret.

I am thankful, she said. My life has run much smoother than I had deserved. . . . My music was a great delight. I had Faith Shenstone for a pupil then.

Austin could not command his look of surprise.

Oh, Austin, she said at length, it was cruel; so I felt it at first. You had blotted me out. Never once, even in fair friendliness, had you mentioned my name.

But —

No. It was I who was wrong. I was wrong to have said it. I love her now, first for Mary's sake, now for herself. Mary had a foreboding in parting with Faith that she would not see her again. That is what she referred to. Poor little girl she has thought of her every day.

Is she so very delicate?

Mary? Yes, Austin. She is full of hope generally and the mind reacts on the body. That spirit is too keen though, Austin. At nights she is feverish often and flushed, pale at times, she is, and lies there so patiently. Oh, Austin, if you knew how dear she is to me.

Mary and Martha returned. The heat had been too much for the little girl, Martha had spread a shawl for her to lie in the shade awhile, but her spirit was too active to let her rest, and she was at length tired out with play.

The cheek was now pale and wan.

* * * * *

The days passed on.

When it was cold, for the weather changed quickly, it was pleasant to sit all together. Mary liked to read out of a great book of travels full of pictures. She used to build her own pictures of lands and rivers and mountains far away, and would listen to Martha's stories by the hour.

Martha was knitting industriously. Austin sat by. Mrs. Neville was playing the pieces she had taught him to like long ago.

Come, let us go out, it is too cold for Mary to-day but we will bring wild flowers back, little girl. I will try to find more shades even of yellow than you managed to bring home last day.

* * * * *

I speak calmly he said to the mother, because I have thought it all out. They had been walking long and talking of old days, and Mrs. Neville thinking of it all had been unable to control her feelings. She was weeping, and he had taken her hand.

I have wronged you. That is past. Our path is now clear.

For what? she quickly questioned.

Marriage.

No, Austin. I too see clearly and I am resolved. This I expected to hear. You have not spoken from reason, not even from feeling. You have yielded to duty, self-denial, not love. No, Austin. This I say firmly. Your esteem I would win. The years that have passed have left too deep their traces on me.

And a smile illumined the face for a moment.

But hear me.—No, no—he cried impetuously, as though to drive on his will, as though to overwhelm her by the fury of passion—himself fearing the onset of a passion more strong. He advanced; but she retreated.

No, no.

For the child's sake. For the child's sake. My heart has gone out to her in love. For her sake, for Mary's sake, for our child.

Austin, her sake would be a bond to hold us all together. That might have been once. But—Austin, I tell you solemnly, she will not remain with us long.—Oh God, my sweet child, my little darling.

These words came to him, unprepared. The thought was ever present with her. He looked at her sadly, in silence, took her hand and pressed it to his cheek.

No, he said, as they returned to the house, you must not talk like that. You are now a little strained that's all. We will speak of it again. Come, all will be well.

* * * * *

Not from mere weakness had she spoken though.

Day by day little Mary grew weaker now. She had caught a chill; a fever seemed to feed on her. Day by day he hoped against hope, and at night with brooding heart lay down. Mary bore her illness patiently. She used to smile and say she was very happy and would soon be well again. There was a peculiar thoughtfulness about her. She seemed to seek to cheer them up.

Austin and Mary and Mrs. Neville had been talking long together looking at the sunset. Martha tired with nursing had gone to bed. The sun had now quite sunk, but still they all three gazed into the west. The quiet dusky light, the stillness, influenced thoughts that were deeper, finer, than those the gorgeous sunset had brought. No word was spoken. The only sound was the ticking clock. Its monotony was grateful. Austin was standing a little in front and wrapped it seemed in his own thoughts. Mrs. Neville glanced at him occasionally and oftener at Mary, whose gaze too seemed fixed, almost strained in its intense expression, on the dusky far-off landscape now becoming dim.

It is getting dark, now, said Mrs. Neville.

The tone of her voice—so gentle—trembled through Austin's frame.

It is getting dark now, Mary. Shall we light the lamp?

No, not just yet, dear Mama. Yet a little while longer, let me look upon this scene.

She spoke in a peculiar voice almost as though to herself.

Her eyes were unaverted, her whole frame, even to the folded hands, was still. Her face was very sweet. They both stood a little back as they watched her. The shadows had gathered now. Mary lay where the light was clearest. The others were half enveloped in the darkness. She was alone with her communion.

* * * * *

Suddenly her features were drawn as with pain; her face became white.

The mother observed it at once.

You are a little weary now, Mary, are you not? she said.

Yes, Mama, a little. Close the blinds now and light the lamp. Do you know, Mama, that when the blinds are drawn and when the lamp is lighted and when we sit together in this little room, the whole world seems completely shut out from my mind; and as I lie and think I can people my own worlds. This little room too seems itself a world, where every object talks to me. I seem to know, Mama, what you wish to say before you speak, and I seem to feel the very movements of your dress. Is that not strange?

Yes, my child. But do not make yourself distressed now, Mary.

It does not pain me, Mama, to think so, or to feel so. No, for when I look upon your face then and feel your hands touching mine, there is something that seems to fill me with its warm comfort; and when your cheek presses mine, and your lips kiss me, there is something that seems to struggle within me, a feeling as though something I cannot grasp at, so fine, and yet that seems to rise, beyond my strength—Is that what they call Love, Mama?

Yes, Mary.

Mary drew a deep sigh, and the little frame trembled and fluttered as the breath escaped. Her thoughts had now taken another range. Presently looking up seriously she spoke to Austin.

Would you be prepared to die? she questioned gravely. Lately I have sometimes felt as though it would not be so difficult as I used to think. Almost as though I could sink into a gentle sleep. Only never again to wake. The tears had filled and blinded Austin's eyes as Mary had begun to speak. He struggled to command himself, but his feelings came in surges. The mother's face alone restrained him. She was calm. Her own feelings seemed to have vanished in her duty.

Austin paced the room. She shall not die. She shall not die, he cried in anguish. She shall not die. But again the tears gushed to his eyes. The mother looked to him. Her look was high and calm, and she raised her hand slightly as though in admonition.

Be still for her sake, she whispered in Austin's ear.

He came to Mary's bedside and knelt beside the bed. Then looking up his face was clearer and showed no sign of conflict.

He took her hand and spoke and his voice too became firm as he continued.

Do not talk of Death, sweet child, he said such thoughts are not for you. You are too young. You—see, Mary, you are a little tired just now, that's all. But when the day is warm again, and the sun shines bright and the sky is blue, Mary, think of that, we will go long walks together in the bush, and hear the birds singing, and pluck the dainty wild flowers, and gather the heather with the bells of fresh pink and white, and bring it home in heaps. And when you are tired then, Mary, we will rest awhile under a great tree where the shade is, and the sky will be blue above and great fleecy clouds will come floating and sailing, and we will sit there and watch them, and trace shapes and figures and faces and grand statues all worked in the beautiful white. And when we look into the still pond at our feet with its surface with not a ripple we will see there too, right down, far down, arching again, another Heaven with its beautiful blue sky and the fleecy clouds.

Yes, yes, said Mary, I have often loved to trace them out. Faith and I often used to sit in the woods and watch them and I would see something and say it was like a sleeping crusader with his great sword across his chest, but Faith would say she could not make it out at all, and she believed it was more like a Polar bear. And Mary smiled and pouted.

That wasn't fair of Faith at all to say so. I'm sure it must have been a crusader though, for Polar bears don't carry swords.

And Faith will come with us too when we go out for walks, and Mama too, won't that be good? And as we hear the birds singing in the blue sky, Mary, we will forget everything but what is beautiful.

Mary drew a sigh and her face grew wistful; the lips a little trembled. She closed her eyes.

Mary will go to sleep now a little, said the mother.

She passed her hands with the tenderest touch round the forehead and down her cheeks. The child's face was composed and soon her regular light breathing showed that she was asleep.

They watched her in silence. Austin would not let himself think of the worst. She will be better yet. She will be better, he kept saying, and he clung to the hope even while the life was ebbing.

*　　*　　*　　*　　*

The mother was calm. Afterwards, in long years afterwards, when Austin had become a living toiler in the great world, when all the manifold thoughts and feelings and experiences that make a life rose up in array, that face with its high, calm expression came upon his mind, and with its gentle power chastened him. Her mind at this hour was greater than his, her spirit finer. The two beings whom she had loved better than her own life, she saw departing from her now. For their sake, oh what a thought for her to think, that may have been the best.

Day by day, and night by night, he knew as their eyes met in that still little room, the love for Mary had absorbed her life.

Through the days, through the long nights her tears had flowed in grief known to her alone. Feelings of goodness had sprung up with that, silent, sacred.

* * * * *

Mary's sleep was not a very long one and the monotonous ticking of the clock was the only sound that broke the stillness of the room. She awoke and the look gave Austin hope.

I was tired, Mama, she said, now I am rested, and—Mama, some drink.

The mother brought a drink of milk to her. She drank a little.

See, she said, showing to Austin the little

mug, it is not glazed. The milk always seems to taste better so. I had a little mug like this, so quaint it is, and broke it, and was very sorry; and Mama found me another just like it. I believe she searched nearly every shop in Dudley. Naughty Mama. She pouted and then took her mother's hand and pressed her lips to it, and lay back again.

Soon again the little form began to tremble and flutter.

She seemed distressed with thoughts that she could not express. She held up her hands a little, and said, Kiss me, Mama.

Her mother kissed her hands, kissed her lips, and kissed her forehead.

Mary sighed. The pupils of her eyes seemed to have expanded, and the shaded eye was looking up with tender pity. Austin's head had been turned aside. Mary was looking at him with great earnestness. He turned and their eyes met. The same light streamed from both.

All that was brightest, all that was beautiful in himself, he saw reflected there. She lifted up her hands again.

His feelings were ineffable. He took the hands and knelt beside the bed. The gentle hands seemed to understand him. He looked up, she held her lips. He kissed them, and with reverence her forehead. The little hands trembled, the eyelids quivered, then again the eyes were wide open, and again their look met his own. He bent, he kissed, turned away; the stemmed feelings rushed in a wild passion upon his mind, and with form shaking and with face convulsed the tears gushed and flooded from his eyes. Gently the mother drew him away. There was no reproof now in her look. Mary's eyes were closed once more. The breathing was regular, fainter, fainter. The mother's eyes were strained upon the dying child. Her ears had sense but for one sound, the faint and fainter palpitation of the breath.

She is dead. The breath had ceased. The clock struck one, two, three . . . twelve.

Austin stood gazing almost in stupor on the face, the colour had not fled, the features were beautiful. They had lost their pain; now all composed. The faintest smile seemed to linger, seemed to dwell on the lips. He strove to command himself, to struggle with his grief. He could not summon thought.

The mother's tensioned feelings had given way;—tears such as those alone can know broke forth whose hearts of life and love have burst in the shadow of this Presence. Austin was standing motionless, gazing blankly forward as though on vacancy.

She took his hand, his touch responded to hers, he grasped her hand tightly. She was kneeling and the pressure of her hand seemed to bring him too to kneel. He obeyed mechanically.

Austin, let us pray, she said.

Whither? whither? said he vaguely, unregardingly, not as though in answer to her question.

She prayed in silence, with deepest reverence—prayed to the Creator Father of all; prayed in the faith which she had recognized and did not question; prayed to her Redeemer. She spoke to herself of His sacrifice, spoke to herself of a meeting beyond the grave, where sorrow is not and the weary spirit finds its rest.

* * * * *

Martha came into the room noiselessly. A glance showed her all, and throwing herself upon her knees beside the mother she gave herself up unrestrainedly to grief.

Then Mrs. Neville rose and beckoned Austin too.

A mist was before her eyes, a strange stillness was at her heart. I must speak to you now and for the last time, and putting on her cloak and bonnet she accompanied him out of the house.

Austin, she said calmly, as they walked in the garden, I wish to say to you what you will think of afterwards.

Do not look behind, look onward. You are young, your spirit is ardent, it will drive you on. Happy, Austin, you will only be where that spirit, that action, ambition, impel you along a course where the road broadens, and where the path leads ever onward. Your passions still can rage like devils. Yes, with a more burning fury, a wilder desperation, now. You hold them with a firm control.

That struggle, that longing for something better than denial, that inexorable suppression; I see it written in your face. It has made you resolute and daring, but these may miss their proper mark. That struggle, that victory has not been fought for nothing, and your life is crying out almost in bitterness to find that higher solace of which this is but the coarser soil. Listen to this too. The law is given. "Thou shalt not" and if this stern law binds us, it can bring no consolation.

We cannot live on this alone. To hate evil, to defy it, and for ever fight this battle, that is our duty; but that struggle too is solved by setting our minds upon the good that is in life, to make that our familiar, so that our natural impulses are turned to that. Well . . . Why now I've been preaching a sermon.

Look, said he, I have seen traits of character in some curious ways. I have seen men plodding away in the even tenor of their lives, for whom standing in their presence one would have felt perhaps not knowing why, deep feelings of respect; men who could face death unflinchingly; men who the higher their opportunity, the higher would they rise; men of warm natural generosity, and warmth of heart. And I have seen deeds of heroism done.

But I think that the best at once and most difficult of tasks is to follow on in daily service, without reward or with reward, calmly, the way of duty.

It is the renunciation that we can make in silence, whose sacrifice we day by day can see that tries us. And I have known a woman who could do this—who loved one whom she painted in her mind far brighter than he was, and felt how dear to her even the sound of his voice, the touch of his hand, felt this even in her tears, but in the silence of her mind concealed what her heart was panting to express; and when she might see that he knew not of this sacrifice, could grow cool to her, nevertheless, with her secret now doubly dead, would find in the hopes of his happiness, reward. Could you believe that such a one could be, he said and looked intently on her face. You must speak. Could you do that? Answer me.

Austin, I love you in my heart's core, and now let that pass for ever. This is the last time, and I am strong now. Beware.

Austin, she said after a long pause, I have a strange charge to give. Go straight now from this house. Do not enter again. Let this talk, Austin, be our last. I will go to my mother's sister. She is a good woman and does good deeds in the district where she lives. I will find relief in that. I will be happy—in thinking—that—in the future, —*you* will be happy. And you, Austin, when I speak of the future, whose image rises? Of whom am I thinking now?

She looked at the desperate eyes.

In your delirium, Austin, you were calling her name.

No, no. That can never be. I must shut that out. My thoughts must never injure her. She's another's.

No, no, said Mrs. Neville. And she told

Austin of Faith's life, her goodness, her hopes, her dreams, and aroused in him again the spirit of old resolves.

* * * * *

Yes. There is my fate, he said. All, she must know all.

No, no. Think, Austin. Her happiness you will destroy with your own—purposeless. I—have I not suffered enough? She will hate me. Let the dead past bury its dead. Her faith in you—

That faith must be surer built up. Devious my way has been. Yet, defeated, obscure, I strove up to this light. Truth is most sacred of all. She cannot hate you. Me— as I am, so I must speak to her.

And now in the first grey breaking of dawn. Good-bye.

* * * * *

He was gone.

She had been resolute. She had done her task.

She had felt his kiss on her forehead. She had smiled as in hope to him, when he uttered the words, good-bye. Unreal they seemed. He departed. Till he was gone out of sight she watched, face blanched, like a statue, motionless. The frightful pain as though of something wherein life dwelt rent from her breast was choking her. How often in the last few days had she felt, in anticipating what had come to pass, the struggling of a wild cry to her lips, the strange urging, tingling through her frame, as if with some fearful scream to fling out of her ablaze the passion of her grief. The reality had come. She had conquered. She had held and crushed down her passion in the power of the will. Now! She turned to the door of the room wherein the dead child lay, the chamber of sanctity, and fell at the entrance swooning, her hand raised, as appealing—for mercy, forgiveness.

The chattels distribute, spend well,
My life is now ended.

BETWEEN TWO LIVES.

CHAPTER XII.

MONTHS had passed away. Months of toil for the poor scholar.

"The Dynamics of the Feelings" was under way again. His aims and his means in this at least were clear to him. He toiled, stemming back all thoughts but his goal in view. He toiled with the earnestness of a man seeking by a good work to win out his own redemption. He saw continually Mrs. Neville's pale face, he heard her sweet voice bidding him march onward, he beheld the beauty of his own child, he gazed on the lids quivering with the last struggle of life.

Remorse availed not. He looked upon his own life. How pure how inextinguishable his hopes had burned. Through what fatal steps had he been cast from his ideals. He had been smirched in the fearful slough of vice. Good God, how horrible it was—those filthy troughs in which the unerect have wallowed and still are wallowing. By years of ardent toil and noble purposes he had sought to rub out, to burn out, the spots of that pollution. How vile the flippancies, the coarseness, the cowardly hearts, the abject servitudes, the unambitious souls. In all moods of a dilatory mind—there is sin. Not in a world of future pain is our hell, but intrinsically in every act of baser life. The sequence is unfaltering. Has sin another meaning, any mystery but this? All is sin that in the supreme scope tends to corruption and to pain. Austin had transgressed; the punishment had struck him its unerring stroke. Still another pain was yet to be meted out, the task most hard. So it seemed to him, when through this atmosphere there came to his mind the image of Faith.

Had Faith changed much? Did she remember him still? Poor Faith, the grey mist hung over her landscapes.

A good discipline it was, the dull round of her daily tasks. In cheerful godliness she walked her path. The wild rebellious heart heard duty's call, obeyed; if sad at times, that was her own secret.

It was in Tarylvale that the days of Faith Shenstone's life were gliding by. Many considerations had advised return.

And there too, the "Dynamics" well in hand, came Austin for a holiday to Mrs. Gray's.

That lady seemed to think Faith a very good girl, self-willed it appeared though, too self-contained.

Faith had already disappointed her mother, grieved her much.

Austin's old friend Kithdale Brown was the last she had rejected.

Kithdale had carried out his plans, was steadily settled, was a very good fellow, and good looking too. She might well have said

" yes." Kithdale took the mild rebuff bravely, planned to work up his practice still more, to get a more handsome turnout, take lessons in singing—for he was told he had a very good voice—run for the Shire Council, and ask her again next year.

For Austin himself Mrs. Gray had more interest, and questioned him much on spiritual things. He gradually found this. Where he was resolved, her adhesion was firm; where he hesitated, she was in doubt; where long arguments lay in the way, he must gain her by dogma, point blank.

He told her of the fate of his hopes, the "Dynamics."

Nevertheless, said the sister, soothingly, mistaking his look, to know that you have done your best, that you have worked conscientiously and merited success, is a recompense for that.

No! he cried, looking up laughing. Good little woman. Your sex, Jessie, seem to like the pensive mood. Your sympathies come then into play. No, no, I am what I am, not what I might have been.

He picked up a ragged looking flower from the bush.

This should have been a perfect rose, but the winds and the rain, or the ripening sun, or the gardener's care, or what other matters may affect their tender lives, have not been favourable to this.

Deprive a man of sight by a stroke from heaven, or the martyr's fate, and he will see no more. Aristotle, the zealous never looked through a telescope. Inexorably he was no astronomer; nor Epicurus, a chemist. Give me my laboratory. Chlorine, I can make; or heroism or murder.

Take your field broad enough,—and you can make of a murderer, a martyr, or of a hero, a slave.

Not in the decalogue merely is evil forfended.

All that delays our progress is evil, all that lessens our lives is sin. Body and mind we must ever repair, fight against forms of their sickness. Resolution to this is the only healthy drift of repentance.

My healthy lungs helped my spiritual

growth; the lack of pence continually sadly hindered it. Be it so. The sum total of what I have done to the end, this only can I throw into the judgment scale.

And here am I, after years of desperate toils, years of obloquy, disadvantage, unnumbered disappointments, renunciations, finding that even in the elevation of my thoughts, as far as I had thereto striven, have I, in a material world, been led into snares; that that simplicity, which had seemed to me to be an attribute of greatness, with which I had hoped to have conducted my life, has starved even the purpose of my development; that a thousand noble feelings and displays, of which indeed once I felt the springs so exuberant, have been almost doomed in the moral desert of my pilgrimage; and that whereas I had placed the sincerity and energy of my mind above the values of show and ostentation, pomp and noise, now, flinging aside ten thousand rules of guidance, and the influence of much that we speak of as education and culture (but which is often really but a devastation of the mind, a scattering of its integrity) I am gathering from my own experiences, even from my failures, admonitions that I feel are now summing up to irresistible dictates. So let it be, for it is unmanly to repine. Nevertheless one cannot help speculating, said Austin, as he talked interminably to his sister. And in reviewing the fields of life, as they passed in wonderful vistas through his mind, he felt time and again, the great onrushing sweeps of emotion as endless possibilities arose, and then the tender, painful, ineffable wistfulness as each successive vista had faded. He smiled at his own desultoriness, weighing the strength of the thoughts that he felt were urging on to the crisis of his life. The warmth of the day made it pleasant simply to sit on the grass, doing nothing, and there was something hypnotic in the even roll of his voice. . . . There is the whole world of woman's influence to be thought of, disruptive though it undoubtedly is to great and serene meditations. For within that sphere are to be found the thousand forces—beauty, refinement, grace, social distinction, as well as all manner of follies and superficial brilliancies, amusements, pleasures, pretensions, fantastic tricks, which yet sweep away the minds of the crowd, and even upon the ambitious keep playing with incessant irritations of vanity, jealousy, pride, and the appeal to all manner of passions reckless and deep. And within that sphere too is to be found the passion of love. For who is there whom it will not stir immensely, even now, the recollection of those kisses that have thrilled through one's soul as though a bold note had been struck, had throbbed through one, from a wonderful musical instrument, hitherto hardly yet tested? Who has not known the kisses that have shaken him to the foundations of his life until all life seemed summed up into one profoundest emotion? Ah! those were the moments to die, for no other emotion, no sentiment, no impulse, no hope, and no fear, lay beyond the supreme and strange pride that rose in that hour.

Mrs. Gray had long lost the sense of this discourse.

Always following the ideal, she said somewhat vaguely. You used to call the poets, Apostles of Nature.

Yet my house is built now on secular things, said Austin rising and pacing about, my devotion is more circumstantial. It seems to me here; truth is the innermost kernel of all that is great.

We are always neophytes. Our temple is not a perishable tabernacle but God's world; its sect wherever faithful minds are found to work; its service is the search for truth; its sacraments the enjoyment of the gifts that nourish sweeter life.

The spirit of thought is the true divine Messenger; it brings tidings of goodwill unto men; the Prince of Darkness quails before this radiant Victor. And there, cried Austin, throwing up into the air his "Dynamics of the Feelings," there is the workshop of a new Republic. Would that our Father could have lived to this day. He had forgiven me all, beholding all my love and all my hate beating into the heart of his Democracy. And, in this hope, O scion of the elder race, thou hadst borne thy fetters lightly. O elder race,

O ancient time, O twilight shapes, gigantic, obscure! Behold the broad coming of the day, opening in its glorious strength, of large splendour, easy, full of cheer. Behold the heaven of these skies, the earth, the sea, the rivers, the fields, accessible, familiar; behold the race of happy children. Ye have stood on the brink of a golden age,—fading with the shadows. Ye have heard the bugle of Liberty peal into an opening world. There is a joy in this that reaches up to worship.

Yes, we are coming to it. For I am just now filled with the thoughts of a thousand experiences in worlds outside the range of orthodox science; the daring leaps of fancy; the delight in warm, vigorous, palpitating existence; the onrush of wild, noble passions, clad in their purple and gold; the bold dynamic movements of the soul; the exquisitely tender touches; the soft luminous expressions, the indefinite ten thousand shades; the compass and sweep throughout the range of feeling, emotion, and passion. Why be wise and sit in a corner? Even our own development will suffer if we do not join in with the turmoil of life, foolish though in great part we esteem it. For the world is by no means conducted on any plan of being directly swayed by the truth of our doctrines or the reasonableness of what we may esteem great principles. Our whole scheme of morals, our laws, etiquettes, and apophthegms are after all but the vague indications of judgments that have been found to be tolerably safe. In the actual world the lines of demarcation are overridden. We must live as well as think, taking the world—which our scheme has but vaguely defined—taking the world in its grossness and its blindness all in good spirit, happy indeed if but our little machinations and scanty purview are not swept away by some superior cataclysm beyond the scope of our prudence and power.

Yes, our standards always come down to that, the earth, and the sky, man's struggle in the natural world. Thanks then to Zeno, and thanks to Epicurus. Seek our standards not in dogma, but in genial apprehension of Truth; nor is the line of duty, of commandments hard and fast, for that is not found at all in Nature.

Not categorical imperatives are the way of life, O Kant. The "Everlasting Yea" be our abiding place. There is bondage in the "Everlasting Nay," and our struggles are but those of the exodus. For what does God want with us? Surely to be men. Our star-struck eyes, our sore-distraught ravings —are they a solace unto Him. Your Kants, your Schopenhauers, even your Fichtes, your Carlyles, the glare of ten thousand lesser lights, seem often to show us but mere juggleries, grand prestidigitation of bizarre emotional effects. Religion? Yes, but wherefore mummery. Scriptures?—we have them everywhere, the serene words of science, the noble passion of an overflowing heart; the green fields, the hills, the forests, the habitations of men are its sanctuaries and temples; every sincere forward marching soul is its priest.

Find the holy spirit where we can, omnipresent, in the storm, in the blue sky, in the roots, the streams, in the glad tones of brotherly help, in the sweet words of love, the imprinting every hour in good deeds.

The gods of the Greeks, let them be symbols, phantasies; their leaping spirits be not lost to us in larger worlds and purer life.

And whither do we march? When I consider my days, looking back, the figure of Death attended me always, sombre, persistent, until I looked upon Death as my arbiter, adviser. Death—it is the supreme hour I said. Our life is but a probation for that. Now, I cry—it is the most inept hour. It is the last act of the decay that steals our faculties, one by one. For the rest cast out its worthless menace. Life is the arbiter. And where is the kernel, that "chief intensity." . . . Jessie, this is a great secret. I am about setting out now to find—the Fountain of Perpetual Youth!

*   *   *   *   *

Infinite is the inner life; dull the symbols of the outer world.

Austin had come to see Faith.

The meeting that the cumbering years

delayed would pass with a cold handshake.

Only a few inches of space intervened, and dull material obstacles.

Mysterious alchemy of force that runs its course when form and feature meet the mutual glance of eyes!

He looked out of the window as though facing his doom.

She, dissimulating, sedulously unconcerned, laughed at her fluttering heart not unashamed.

In vibrating balance, supple, a moment she stood, drew a breath and opened the door.

Confused with the light from his eyes, she lost her self-possession and tripped.

He caught her. The cheeks felt the warm flush of life, the lock-up lips quivered, the eye could not pale its fire.

Austin! Faith! They stared at each other in wonderment.

* * * * *

Days, weeks even, passed away before Austin spoke to Faith again, though he had glimpses of her occasionally. He seemed, even to himself at times, to have lost comprehension of his own mind, its mysteries, its endeavours. Wandering over the hills, sitting book in hand under the shade of the trees, or strolling, alone, unembarrassed and free " tarrying and talked to by tongues aromatic," he filled up the measure of the livelong day. He was still young and the dream of love was sweet—then again came revulsion and pride.

Mrs. Gray and Faith were slowly walking in the garden together when unexpectedly Austin emerged on the path. He had looked wildly round for a chance of escape, then drew himself up like a stag at bay.

Faith, come hither, child. You are an interesting being. Your mind is serious and strong, that countenance is turned to grave things, but, Faith, the lightness of your step has a little witchery therein; I love the dimpling of your cheek when the smile ripples the surface, the carriage of the head, the steadfast eye. Sweet Faith, he said, half laughing, truly you are little lower than the angels.

Mrs. Gray had departed to see about the tea, and Faith, in no mood to be laughed at, she said, inquired whether she had not better leave him again alone with his books, one whom, she added maliciously, travel had made so superior!

Yes, I have looked into books, and have bent my head in reverence, and have seen the solid fabrics of a nation's wealth; the pomp and pageantry, and gilded masks—yet, said he, laughing again, this is very sweet, this rare delight of health and peace, I see around. Fragrant is the garden, clear the sky, the landscape rich with colour, the Woady Yalloak streamlet flowing on to the dark blue hills of the Woady Yalloak range, the burning colours of the sunset, the crimson, the mountains and the fields of the gorgeous crimson, and the deep sombre clouds, the dim-basalt walls, the battlements, and there the blazing gates of Heaven's demesne.

Faith, you are a sweet girl, come hither, child, your cheeks are like the blossom of crab apples, your lips like the red heather, song seems to sparkle and hang from them and to be cast forth, like, what shall I say, like the spray from the mountain side! like the falling of refreshful rain. You are a sweet being. A fragrance is on your brow, —on your hair—a nimbus. Human beauty— it is the fairest triumph of earth. And, Faith, thou art beautiful.

The day was soon to be of the past.

They stood together in the garden hand-in-hand, and the light winds brought the perfume of the flowers, and in the freshness of the day Faith's eye—a godly cheerfulness, its light—looked on the blossoms, bright and chequered, of the trees, the shrubs, the sober tints, wandered along—the old familiar scene yet ever renewed—the winding flowing stream, round the hill base, across the long flat valley, over to the distant range, out to the vaporous purple of the eventide.

And now the sun had set. And they looked out upon the infinite space, filled with the mysteries of space. The faintest breath of cool refreshing wind had come. The first few stars had peeped out one by one. The world was shut out alike in the stillness and the dusk of night. They stood mute, but not unconscious of each other, children standing on the ocean shore won for awhile from the fret and the care of life, wrapped in the shadowing night, held by the sense of awe.

And now the slight breeze grew fresher, and Austin broke the silence.

Faith, said he, realize it. Each particular star you see is itself a world far greater than our own—that minute and shapeless speck. The myriad worlds roll on in the immensity of space, and the touch of its light has struck upon us here.

Austin, said Faith, and her voice was low, my thoughts have seemed as though I faintly endeavoured to comprehend them, and could not. We seem here the merest atoms too. All our best can do seems to fade away to nothing.

No, replied Austin in the same grave and gentle tone, speak not so. Our life is great around us. These thoughts and feelings are not small to us. The surge of feelings, our impulses, our acts and thoughts, are real, vivid. Yes, he cried, as he flung up his arm and braced himself to the now freshening breeze, even now I can feel their deep resounding music beating on my heart. Why, Faith, doth not this cooling draught bring the keen touch of life. Here is something tangible. The earth has a rude grasp. Courage it demands and a certain firmness of resistance, but there is a grand comfort in its broad enduring structures.

Austin used to come home in the evening radiant and fresh.

Mrs. Gray wondered if this was what he called study, and questioned him as was her wont.

True, I have shown no precipitate haste for books, he replied, but rule may not be order, nor effervescence energy. Here I have felt myself as the husbandman who may sleep, and his harvest grows. Better than to think it is at times, as to me now, to know within myself renewal, fertility. Here I have had the solace of a blessed peace. The air comes to me here wooingly and sweet.

And wandering about, or sitting under the shade of trees, and viewing this familiar landscape my thoughts have moved easily, and with a touch above the plodding and distressful toil there have come, with this fresh health, formative elements; my mind has worked with insight, plastically moulded by a Power that makes these thoughts part of me.

Yes, truly, I have been led on by something higher than me. I have been the gnome of a Power, and what I have esteemed my motives have been but the means of leading to each successive step. I had thought to have found a religion in science, and had filled my mind with the greatness of its total purpose. . . . "I have no time to think of Dion now:" Yes, that was a great saying of Plato's, dignified, serious, serene, when Dion had hoped that Plato would not speak evilly respecting him. It was one of the things that had influenced my way of thought. And again I esteemed Goethe great for his saying, when having asked the news of a friend and that friend had responded by giving the details of some uproar or revolution, I know not, in France. " It is not of these matters I was thinking, but of the revolution in the world of thought, the battle of Cuvier and Geoffroy Saint Hilaire." Cæsar, after all his conquests, looked wistfully towards a greater glory— the discovery of the source of the Nile. And Napoleon, on the voyage to Egypt, gazing up into the starry skies, did he not feel an awe greater than the rapture of the strife, the whirling thought of victory.

These matters gave one pause. And so I was led to the contemplation of the works of great thinkers, Locke, Newton, Young, Schwann, Ampère, Spencer, Darwin, and a hundred others. And as I beheld those movements of energy which have urged on the advancement of our race, and thought of the examples of these men, I esteemed of inferior account the bulk of what fills the pages of history—the devastating tumults of war, the mean chicanery of politics and law, the shallow gossips of courts; and I was inclined to disparage even the personality of the men whom the world has looked upon as heroes.

Yet! not that I have changed in my inward idea, but I have received experiences that have forced me again to turn my eye upon the measure of things. For I have found many scientific men, men whom I have considered ought to have been in the van, true leaders of the people, I have found these men cowardly, petty, and even servile to those shams and farces which their own works had taught me to hold in contempt. The men of knowledge are in fact often dry, severe little personages, absorbed in their own little systematizations and cut off from a hundred realms of greatness, not merely in art, poetry, the charm of personal grace and beautiful intercourse, but also from the nobler passions of the soul, courage, resistance, depth of resolution, magnetic influence, the air of greatness of the antique. Yes, there may be little in the actual pursuit of a scientific life to lead a man to great and generous feelings or give him that fascinating power of a noble and sweet disposition that we may find at times even in those but little instructed.

And, again, after all, or rather at the beginning of all, it is the poetry of science that has led me on, that peculiar feeling of which the dullest feel the promptings, to know the inner working of things, to see the processes of which others see the results, to survey great vistas of human efforts, to behold the most perfect organization of thought, the most refined use of intellectual instruments, to see brought into the world new theories, deep principles, which have made clearer old problems and immemorial puzzles, and which will endure in human knowledge after the ruins of a thousand nations; and lastly, this profound stirring of the mind, to hope to answer the questions: Who am I, whence came I, what here is my task, my duty, whither do I go?

But there is no finality. Even the deepest results of science, the most finely conceived speculations of philosophy remind us again and again of Newton's own comparison of the child picking up shells on the sea-shore.

As each new science is opened up, the prospect that it seems to offer to our hopes is greater than the actual fulfilment. Our final problems and our nearest and our deepest are as far off a solution as ever. Marvellous indeed and vast are the works of modern science, but even on the highest basis of this work one finds that the duty of man is not merely to *know*.

And there is one more regard in which an irresistible feeling rises over me, a fierce dynamic onslaught, in reading again the records of men whose lives have been led on by a sort of sure instinct greater than the indications of temperate judgment. Must we not admit that man of little scruple, Napoleon, into the Pantheon? I feel my heart beat fast at the tale of the daring resolution, exhaustless energy, the quick, infallible decision, the never faltering courage, the mastery of mind, the force of will, the atmosphere of greatness as of one born by right of nature to rule. And above all, he was famous at twenty-seven, while he had youth and beauty, and enthusiasm, and the glory unimpaired of hope, and pleasure, exhaustless verve, and never questioning belief in life. Yes, that was great. Great is the power of personality, *the man himself*, greater perhaps than every other gift of earth, or product of human society. . . . Keats, Spencer, Napoleon, a remarkable Pantheon! Well, the world is here, and doubtless too the touchstone.

Mrs. Gray looked on him with a sort of wonder as he talked.

Jessie, he said, after a long pause I wish you would invite Mrs. Shenstone over next Friday—not Faith though, he added laughingly. That is, I will bring a message myself to Faith?

Mrs. Gray smiled too.

And what about Faith?

Ah, Faith. Yes, she interests me.

Interests you? Yes. I half expected you would have fallen in love with her.

Love! That's a word used here and there. What does it precisely mean? Is there a certain feeling, or is it simply a more interested regard and inclination? It's hard to define that word.

Is it? But about ten years ago you told me you had analyzed it, satisfactorily! Faith's nature I think is rather a cold one, hard even, and reserved. It's unnatural for so young a girl.

Cold? hard? Say, true! Her mind is direct, candid. I like that word. I like her manner. Cold. No. True. That girl could be as true as steel to—that is, I do not think she is cold, if one really knew her.

Very well, Austin, have your way. I rather like Faith Shenstone myself. I don't know what people are coming to. That wretched-looking girl of Thompson's said they didn't want middle-aged married women to help in the decoration of the church! I don't care, it's better to be a young matron than a parchment-skinned girl at any time. As far as looks go, at least I am sure I don't look a day more than thirty, do I now, Austin?

No.

I don't know what people are coming to. You see young ladies of fifteen, forsooth, with all the airs of women of the world. Faith is the only sensible girl I know. I think she's rather nice looking too.

She's beautiful! She's an angel!

Well what do you like particularly about her—

I scarcely know, he replied absently. It is not her beauty, her grace. I'm certain it is not her talents, not even her voice, her manner, not even her character. She's an angel, an angel. I seem to have no other reason to myself than that she is Faith. And he strode off to think out the matter by himself.

Austin! called out Mrs. Gray.

Well?

Austin, you're not in love—because you have not exactly analysed it. But, stay! Austin!

He passed Faith in the garden, bowed sedately to her.

Faith looked after him, when she was sure

he would not notice it, and walked meditatively into the house. Mrs. Gray was still thinking of Austin in particular, and watched the face of the cold Faith as she mentioned his name but got no definite result.

Faith, she explained I can't make Austin out, can you?

No, replied Faith.

He has something on his mind, I do believe. I don't think I ever rightly made him out. He is always acting on some caprice it seems to me, and preaching all the time of prudence, candour, and the like. Is he in love with you, Faith, or not? Did he ever speak of love?

What! Has Austin—

Could you die for him? asked Mrs. Gray, suddenly but laughingly.

The cold Faith remained silent.

Now don't be angry, said Mrs. Gray, laughing, for you know one has to live with him. I'd like to find out what his secrets are. It depends on that. He was reading this book last night and I took it out of his room. See what he has written here.

Is it right to read it?

The book's mine, said Faith.

A gleam came into her eyes. Can it be that he loves— She was herself again and resolved! Give me the book. It will not be wrong if I read it to him. . . . I'll turn the tables this time.

And here is another book that he used to have before he went away. He seems to have been half mad, or in love, or something of the sort, for he has written fearful nonsense. He would be mad enough if he knew I had it.

Then give it to me, said Faith there's no harm if I read it to him. I'll brave his anger. We'll see, if he is going to triumph over people!

CHAPTER XIII.

Austin met Faith full of desperate thoughts. At one time his horizon seemed overcast, murky.

Then again the sun brightened, and his step too lightened, and his heart went singing along.

Poor little Faith was unconscious of this, unconscious too of his presence as he stood at the half-opened door of her parlour and looked into the room. He smiled. Faith in the corner was lost on a flower pot. It was warm, blinds drawn, her hair too was down, a pinafore she wore, and looked girlish. Unconscious, sweet, was the pale patient face.

How good she is, he said. And the touch of admiration held him in check.

She had tended the mignonette, had

smothered her face amongst it, and looked over to the opposite wall contemplatively and cast her eyes towards the ceiling, and raised her hand shading her forehead; and then her thoughts seemed to wander for she drew a deep breath, and turned her head, and started and rose suddenly in wrath. She had blushed to be sure, but this made her warmer.

What do you mean, Austin Brandt, she cried, coming to our house in a fashion like this? And she felt the blushes growing warmer and warmer till she hated him.

I came to speak to you, Faith, he said laughingly then, and advanced.

Back? she cried and slipped away.

Very well. I will wait for you.

Austin took a seat by the window and picked up a book and read patiently; presently Faith appeared again.

Her dress was rather primmer, her hair neatly braided, the warm tinging of her cheek subdued. She looked a sweet Puritan with the steadfast eyes.

She carried a book in her hand, and appeared mistress of her own heart at least.

Well, said Austin, forgive me, Faith, now, will you not? And then we will talk sensibly. Your indignation covered you with pretty blushes, Faith. I came upon a sentimental moment, eh?

You came ill-manneredly enough, said Faith, but you are yourself I see a pretty sentimentalist. She showed the book.

That's infamous, Faith Shenstone, he cried, you have no right to read that.

No, Austin Brandt, and you have no right to come peeping into my room. Faith laughed at his confusion and proposed to read to him.

He looked round the room in despair; then sat with his head on his hands.

This note book, said Faith, is a remarkable affair. I would not have thought you so foolish.

What's this? Myriad constitution of mind. Pathos, Glare of passion, Courage, Airy Humour, practical application of the thoughtful sense. What's that? Madness, longings. Keen flashes of inner light; robust, and earnest action. H'm. But that's not what

I want. That's written years ago. What's this? Estimate for Abutments—Lime concrete, 25s. No—that's not it.

When the youthful heart lays to itself the charge—but that's all old.

Here it is —

And picture thee with thy sweet serious winsome face and take thee by the hand. Thy strength, thy energy, self sacrifice I claim; all that thy life quickens thou must offer up to me. But clasped in my arms, Faith, held by my strength, and cherished in my love, thou hast not merely solace, Faith; thine heart is nourished with a newer life.

Great Heavens! he cried out, furiously red. Stop! I never wrote that —

Yes, you did, and this too. Are you my ideal? Surely not. The cold, haughty, little Faith, and wilful too. My ideal would have been something quite other, I think. I don't know that ever I had an ideal, but I know, my sweet little Faith, that you are better than my ideal. Every natural touch, your step, the tones of your voice, the little locked-up lips, the look of those steadfast eyes as they looked at me, all have come to me now and made me know how much I loved you. O to have seen you once again, to look into my little darling's eyes again, to feel—the pressure—of her hand.

Her voice had trembled—and with a sudden strange lowering broke.

He leapt up. Her eyelids drooped; he took her hand in his. She could not look up. She struggled to resist but the trembling had got the better of her. There seemed to be no tension.

A cloudy unreality invested her, she seemed to float on billows but with no direction yet. She felt his arm around her waist, felt the hot look upon her face. She was swept unresisting away.

Yes, Faith, he cried, I love you, I love you. My darling, my darling. He kissed her.

Yes. Say that you love me, Faith. Let me hear the words again—again. Let them fall into my ear and burn like molten gold. Kiss me, sweet Faith, I cannot comprehend the words. Words would separate us, Faith. Your warm cheek is real. Sweet Faith, kiss me.

She demanded to be free, but his face was all gentle now and he pressed her hand softly to his cheek and to his lips.

Nay but hear me, Faith, he said. You little know when long ago I separated from you, when you were still a girl how much you had slipt into my mind. Strange are the workings of our feelings. Their motions sometimes seem to baffle reason, yet even then I loved you as I do now. You did not know the struggle separation cost me, the victory that left all my possessions barren. I departed with thoughts greater than I could contain. And then by hour and day, and often waking in the night and hearing the tempest roaring far far away from Faith, I thought of you. Leaning over the ship's bow and looking down into the water—how the vessel rushed along and the billows that were left behind were bearing me away from you. New faces, new modes of life, new skies, they all brought me back to the old. Then with the years between I could in spirit have flown to you in the moment and clasped you as now to my heart, and these hours must deepen into the strain of days, the days grow to weeks, stretch to the long years that absorb our life. There was a loneliness about my heart. Mad impulses that almost burst the fibres of my soul, that I will never think of more, swept over me. Then came grief, and news of death. Then at last with the slow moving cycle that rolls the years into the eternal silence the days were come when I again could turn my eyes to this our land of sunshine and of liberty. And then again the ship and the long swell of the world embracing ocean, the tract of waste waters. . . . We had often music on board. Its wizard touch threatens to sweep the longings of our minds beyond the compass of its vain attempt.

And then again as I lay awake at times in the dark night, and the monotonous billows dashed against the ship, your image came too often to my mind. The struggle was cruel.

He let her hand go and walked about the room, and Faith stood looking at him, wondering. He did not seem to be regarding her at all. He took a seat by the table opposite to her and she sat down too and looked at him. He smiled. Faith, could you still walk 20 miles a day?

With you, Austin!

And you love me, Faith?

Yes, Austin.

He smiled again gravely, he looked at her but with no immediate recognition in his eyes.

A few moments and the shock would come. A world of bright awakening life had streamed in with her touch; that would vanish like a dream, the dull blank of a life bereft of meaning would be his. This or a better stroke?

Now as he looked at her and she thought he was not regarding her, his mind was dwelling on the days when he knew he loved her first. The words, Yes Austin, made him smile—direct as a sabre cut, prompt as a soldier on duty, or the giving of a cup of cold water in the name of a prophet. It brought back the picture of Faith the day the saddle girths of her horse had broken, and she had fallen, and he had run to pick her up, and cried Are you hurt, Faith? and she had answered, No, Austin.

When the buggy was nearly overturned, and he had asked her if she had been alarmed she had answered, No, Austin.

And when he had talked of himself to her, and asked her if he should go, she had answered, Yes, Austin.

He had smiled at these answers then and he smiled now.

He beheld the supple form, with Nature's benison of health therein, and looked into the pale patient face, as he called it, though not very pale, and the little locked-up lips that yet could smile in witchery, and the clear steadfast eyes, beneath whose depths were radiant mysteries. And Faith was shading her forehead with her right hand now, while her left was folding down assiduously the dogear of a book.

And did you think of me so far away? Was it not hard to retain one in mind whose feelings, thoughts and struggles, during the time that had passed were all unknown to you?

No, Austin, do not say that, she replied in simple candour, how could I forget? Sometimes Mama and I would talk of you and I would remember you as you were. And— and then I knew you would come back. It was long to wait, it was hard to bear, but I knew I would see you again.

The eyelids opened over soft eyes, and drooped again gently.

The tone again—she spoke slowly and softly as though half musingly—came to him with a newer apprehension. For the first time, subtly as light coming over the darkness of a landscape, he saw at once revealed her life and peculiar task. A higher understanding was awake; he knew the burden of the secret through the years, kept close within, sung ever to herself, through dismal outward silence. The patient duty of her daily life he knew, the faith and maiden love that in her soul was sacred, quickening now in firstlings of its hopes.

A look of meaning passed like a beam of light between them.

A gloom deepened on his features. He paced the room.

Faith did you ever picture me as frivolous,

morose, perhaps flippant? No, no, no, not flippant, I hope. But Faith—there was a time when a fever burned within me, and without a guide, without an aim, I faltered, —and—

She had hung her head, he had come to her, and he took in his hand the locket she wore on her breast. He had opened it and beheld Mary's portrait. His voice had become husky, he could not go on.

She felt that agitation. She looked up, and the deep flush of shame rushed over his face; a swift glance from the locket to him— a wild cry, and she reeled, hid her face, fell.

* * * * *

He stood looking at her vacantly. Then stooping as though to raise her, made a slight movement forward.

No! no! she cried, and the sobs began to come.

Austin's eyes were fixed on her, and his ears alive to every sound. After a time the sobs became less frequent, her breath more regular, her tears fell, at first bitterly, then, as he knew, with gradual exhaustion and assuagement of grief.

Stooping down he took her hands, held them for a while, then grasping them firmly with a firm voice called —

Faith!

She was sobbing, faintly tried to release her hands. Faith!

She allowed herself, as though by his physical force, to be partially raised. She was kneeling by the table with her face covered. He was calm, but an earnest fire burned within.

This is the deepest hour of my life he said, Faith Shenstone, rise and hear me. The same command as though of superiority was in his voice, and as he raised his hand, she rose, but stood with averted face.

Forgive.

She remained silent.

Speak!

I have no power to forgive or to deny. I am a weak, foolish girl. Spare me. Leave me.

No. We will know each other in this

hour, Faith! When I look back, I see how by things whose powers I would have scorned my actions have been formed. Out of this I raised myself. Even while the enemy had held me, out of this I raised myself, and strove upward. First the bitter draught of remorse, then the struggle against what wound me as in a net, with no solace, no encouragement, but my own resolves in secret, and the inward whispers which urged my upward way, the energy, the strength of will.—Sickness lay in the way too, and failure; and my soul was hungry and eager.

There was a loneliness in this, Faith. I knew then the deep significance of innocence. Let me speak to you as a woman now, and your answer will determine to you in the great field of life, the tasks and struggles in our march onward, all that makes a life. I have sinned; must my life be blasted, that trust which my powers have given me be gone for ever, sunk in the records of a withered past. No, no. But I would have it from your heart. See, said he placing her pot of mignonette where she saw it, but did not look at him. This flower, which your own hands have tended, how sweet its perfume, and its form how very delicate; tender yet fostered to an exquisite perfection. This fragrance and this delicatest form lead us to thoughts that purify the mind.

Yet its roots are deep in the miry earth. It must be tended with incessant care. Neglect will wither it. Your care, Faith, has saved it from decay.

Faith, when first I saw you, you were a little girl, a child slight and delicate, changed by every passing thought, in tears at every cloudy mood; kindly care and love have saved you too, nurtured you too, into all the grace and ripening worth of womanhood. Even now you tremble on the shore of that life in which your lot of womanhood is cast, to bid adieu for ever to your sweet life of girlhood.

Look upon the past; how wistful seems it all, how tender, sad, the dreaming recollection, the thought, Faith, of the days when first you came to know me, the strange picturing of a child's mind. Then again, when first I parted with you, perhaps, to be, for ever, and the subtle links were broken, and you sobbed with the heavy thought of all that separation meant.—

And now here again how wonderful is the growth of spirit and of form. How many defeats, disasters, by how many trials, sorrows, tears, have you passed; and still again, the never ending task anew, but now with growing strength. Day after day brings the familiar round, the mask of things which are wrapped in endless mystery. We heed not, we chase trifles, will o' the wisps upon the precipice's edge. Often in my life, breaking into the dull careless march of trivial things has come the sudden and tremendous stroke that has opened up that gulf—the caverns of for-ever silent Death. Yes, many times I have been close to death. Whether in the sudden peril, or the dread insidious approach, I have borne myself with fortitude. And often in my days of lonely toil in foreign cities, oppressed with the wrongs, the evils, the mad despairs of our race, my past life almost a dream, my future hopes a fairy tale

—I have said, I could die now. It is not hard to die. . . . Such have been my stumblings. And now I see strange, wonderful, the Approaches, through which I have been led to truer life. Not then, in danger in downcast hours did I sink. I knew that I could not die, not until my work was done. A sacred flame had been given me in charge.

Good God where is that charge! Whither does my life lead, whereunto reach? I come back with peculiar bewilderment yet familiarity, wonder and certitude, to those instincts for guidance that impressed me as a child, and make me know that there is but one death to him who follows his true destiny, and that to him who denies it life itself is but a wretched effacement.

THE END.

www.ingramcontent.com/pod-product-compliance
Lightning Source LLC
Chambersburg PA
CBHW021822230426
43669CB00008B/837